THE STATE OF BLACK BRITAIN

Volume Two

by Dr Aaron Haynes

HANSIB

This volume was launched to coincide with the London Borough of Haringey's Race Equality and Community Relations Awards, to mark the European Year Against Racism, 1997

*Dedicated to
my wife Anita*

CONTENTS

FOREWORD by Peter Tucker 9

PREFACE 11

1. THE THATCHER YEARS AND THEIR LEGACY 15
The General Ideological Base • The Destruction of Local Government • The Effect of Privatisation • The Prince and Thatcher • The Judgement

2. FREE MARKET OR SLAVE MARKET 25
Minimum Wage • Black Involvement In the Labour force • Racial Discrimination in Employment • Trades Union Movement and Race • Business Enterprises

3. THE EDUCATIONAL CHALLENGE 39
The National Curriculum • Multicultural Education • The Language of League Tables • Some Areas of Achievement • Racial Harassment • The Collapse of the Youth Service • Higher Education • Self Help and Community Choice • Some Formal Investigations

4. THE HEALTH, SOCIAL SERVICES & WELFARE CRISIS 53
National Health Service • Black Elderly • Mental Health • Child Care Issues • Race and Social Work Training • Housing • Social Security

5. LAW AND ORDER 69
The Criminal Justice System • The Police • The Courts • The Legal Profession • The Prison Service • The Probation Service

6. BLACK PEOPLE & THE MEDIA 87
Racism and the Mass Media • Politics, Race and the Media • Advertising • Complaints • Training • The Black Media • Media Awards

7. THE NEW POLITICS 97
*The Ethical Dilemma • Making the Law Effective • Immigration
and Asylum • The European Dimension • The Case for a Bill of
Rights • The Drive for Political Recognition*

8. THE BLACK AGENDA 2000 109
*The Basic Principles • The Economic Agenda • Privatisation
• A Matter of Government • Dealing with Discrimination
• Law and Order • Education and Employment • Housing
• Health and Community Care Services • Arts and Broadcasting
• Sports and Recreation • Conclusion*

REFERENCES 121

BIBLIOGRAPHY 125

LIST OF TABLES		PAGE
Table 1.	Economic status of people of working age: by agenda and ethnic group. Spring 1995	27
Table 2.	Population by ethnic group and age. Spring 1995	29
Table 3.	Unemployment rates by ethnic group. Spring 1994	30
Table 4.	Nature of discrimination by employers - all respondents feeling unfairly treated by employers	34
Table 5.	Percentage of children meeting Government set norms. 1995	43
Table 6.	Scales of Teachers	44
Table 7.	Black elderly growth in the UK. Within projection to 2010.	54
Table 8.	Families with dependent children by ethnic group. Winter 1994/95	58
Table 9.	Ethnic group of head of household by household size. Spring 1995	63
Table 10.	Ethnic group of head of household by tenure 1993/94	64
Table 11.	Overcrowding: by ethnic group of head of household 1993/94	64
Table 12.	Number involved in Crown Court Study by gender and ethnic group	80

FOREWORD

The black communities in Britain have as a whole moved from being the immigrant communities of the post-war period to second and third generations of primary immigrants who are full citizens of the United Kingdom with all the rights attached to such citizenship. In Volume One of THE STATE OF BLACK BRITAIN, first published in 1983, Aaron Haynes provided an analysis of the push and pull forces that gave rise to the post-war immigration of black people into Britain. He reviewed the development of government policies to cope with an immigrant population, and challenged a number of the underlying assumptions which weakened the effectiveness of the policies and led to the failure of many immigrants to fulfil their aspirations.

Volume Two examines the absence of policies directed at the needs of the black communities, and argues that the Thatcher revolution with its emphasis on individualism and its rejection of community did not only affect white society, but had a traumatic effect on the development of the multi-coloured state of Britain. The gains of the 1970s were slowed down and in some cases put into reverse. The struggle for recognition and acceptance became more difficult and complicated. It was more than the problems of migration and racial discrimination; it was also the challenge of living in a rapidly changing society, experiencing its own crisis of identity.

Haynes argues in this volume that while racial discrimination remains an important issue for black Britain; if the aspirations of the early settlers are to be realised, black people will need to articulate a political agenda based on inclusive politics. And who else is better placed to mark the starting point for that debate than the author with his excellent track record of total commitment to equality of opportunity and the elimination of racial discrimination? He has done just that and, in his usual forthright and sometimes provocative style, also suggested the parameters within which the debate could usefully take place.

This volume will be most useful to the present generation of leaders and aspiring leaders of the black communities in Britain. Old stagers may also usefully browse.

Peter Tucker
The first Chief Executive of
the Commission for Racial Equality

PREFACE

It is now twenty-one years since the last Race Relations Act was passed in 1976. 1997 is also The European Year Against Racism and it seems an appropriate time to produce Volume Two of The State of Black Britain. Like Volume One, it is designed to help administrators, policy makers, professionals and students explore the implications for Black people of a range of public policies as these have developed over the last fifteen years. It also provides an overview for those who seek a general review of the main concerns affecting the practice and delivery of racially sensitive services.

The inclusion of a question on ethnic origin for the first time in the 1991 census has considerably improved our database. Not only have the first results confirmed what we had for years known in broad terms, but they have allowed us to start a more detailed analysis of the relative outcomes for individual ethnic groups. This will become increasingly important in future planning strategies.

In Volume One, I argued that the struggle would be long and that indeed some would die before the journey's end. The Thatcher years have demonstrated just how difficult and how long the struggle is destined to be. Much of the spirit of Black awareness that was evident in the seventies has been sapped out of the community. Some slow and gradual progress has been made, but so too has the emergence of Black on Black violence been witnessed. In the first six months of 1996 more Black people have been murdered by other Black people than were murdered by White people in the two previous years. Many of those murders were believed to be drug related.

While racism remains a major concern for Black people; there are other issues emerging that will demand urgent and direct community intervention if the battle against racism is to be won. It is my fervent hope that the analysis of where the Black community stands now and the agenda recommended for the lead up to the year 2000 will serve to assist in meeting the challenges that lie ahead.

I would like to express my thanks to countless friends, colleagues and students who have helped to shape my thinking over the years. I am indebted to Pamela Steele for patiently typing the manuscript, my wife Anita for carrying out the arduous task of proof reading and my ex-colleague and friend, Peter Tucker for providing the foreword to this volume.

Aaron Haynes

THE STATE OF BLACK BRITAIN

Volume Two

Sir Herman Ouseley, first black Chairman of the Commission for Racial Equality

"If Margaret Thatcher wins, I warn you not to be ordinary, I warn you not to be young, I warn you not to fall ill. I warn you not to get old."

Neil Kinnock MP
Leader of the Labour Party, 1983

CHAPTER ONE

THE THATCHER YEARS AND THEIR LEGACY

THE GENERAL IDEOLOGICAL BASE

Margaret Thatcher is not everybody's favourite politician. But what remains a matter of record is that there are few Prime Ministers this century who have had a greater impact on the nation. What has seldom been realised is the dire effect she had on the Black community in Britain. On the eve of the 1983 general election, Neil Kinnock MP, the leader of the Labour Party, in summing up his election campaign declared. "If Margaret Thatcher wins, I warn you not to be ordinary, I warn you not to be young, I warn you not to fall ill, I warn you not to get old". But he could have added with equal poignancy "I warn you not to be Black".

It was not that she had any specific distaste for any of the groups mentioned by Neil Kinnock nor indeed for Black people. It was simply that she was a conviction politician driven by Calvinist ideological persuasion towards an individualist revolution. She was therefore single mindedly intent on destroying anything that stood in the way of achieving goals which she had convinced herself were for the good of the nation as she perceived it. This meant that she had to make a clean break from the post war Tory consensus of a one nation Britain in which there were shared rights and responsibilities within the ambit of a shared community.

Brian Elliott et al have strenuously argued that what Margaret Thatcher with her intellectual mentor, Sir Keith Joseph, did was to create a platform of real political power for the ideas, policies and concerns of the radical right and thus allow the New Right to change the lives and thinking of a generation of Britons[1]. The new commitment to materialism and the elevation of the every man for himself culture

15

succeeded in widening the gap between the haves and the haves-not. It was a time when the rich got richer and the poor, poorer. This was a dispiriting time for those who as immigrants had been seeking to raise their families from the bottom of the social pile.

Her 1979 victory had been achieved by mobilising and harnessing the various elements of the New Right including the National Association for Freedom, a group that had been very active in breaking the Grunwick strike and who had campaigned during the Wilson-Callaghan period of government against various pieces of legislation designed to strengthen workers' rights. Elliott et al also contend that the National Association of Freedom (NAF) saw such legislation as the employment Protection Act and closed-shop provision as no more than the denial of the legitimate rights of property owners to have full and unfettered control over their capital as well as their workers.[2] The NAF succeeded in bringing the Association of Self-Employed People (ASP) under their umbrella and their united front created a campaign army to the Thatcherite thrust towards a new market economy.[3]

To be successful they had to remove the power of the Trades Union barons. The Tory party had never forgotten Heath's humiliation at the hands of the miners which had lead to the three day week in 1974. They were delighted when the unions, rejecting Healey's five per cent wage limit, had embarrassed the Callaghan government with a series of public sector strikes during what became known as the winter of discontent in 1978/79. This paved the way for the Thatcher victory.

Number one on her hit list was the union stranglehold. The unions had to be tamed. There was a three pronged attack. First legislation. This would limit the right to strike without a ballot, secondary pickets would be banned, mass picketing would be outlawed, employers could seek redress in the courts for damages in calls of unlawful strike action, closed shops would be ended, union leaders would have to face periodic elections and union funds for political purposes would have both to be declared and sanctioned by membership. The legislation was brought in over a period of years in a series of restrictive steps.

The second prong was selected battles with individual trades unions. This was made easy now that secondary pickets were outlawed and unions found it difficult to supply the customary support to weaker unions. With the courts having the power to sequester the funds and other assets of unions who fell out of line, it was game, set and match to Maggie. She was prepared if necessary to destroy the industry if that is what it took to defeat the union. Arthur Scargill and the National Union of Miners were left until virtually the last. Yet despite all the preparation success was due largely to the defection of the Nottinghamshire miners who set up the Democratic Union of Miners, and weakened the resistance.

16

The third and most sinister prong in this attack upon the workers was the creation of a large pool of unemployed. This would operate as a dampener on wage demand and deliver a more compliant even if less satisfied workforce. For a long time the workers most affected were the unskilled among whom a large number of Black young people were to be found. So that while it would be wrong to suggest that Thatcher had targeted Black people, they were none-the-less one of the principal losers in her campaign against organised labour.

One of the quarrels between Thatcher, her successor John Major and the European Union, as illustrated in the conflict over Maastricht, is precisely the perception that the successes against the workers in favour of the employer, particularly the small employers to whom they owe so much, would be reversed under the terms of the Social Chapter.

Another reward to her supporters was to immediately cut the top rate of taxation. The justification being that you had to allow top people to keep more of their money in order to encourage them to work hard and in that way keep producing wealth for the nation. To accomplish this a concerted effort needed to be made on increasing revenue and reducing public expenditure. We shall see how two aspects of this effort were conducted and the impact they had on the well-being of Black people in the society.

THE DESTRUCTION OF LOCAL GOVERNMENT
Local Government became an easy target in the fight to adjust government expenditure. One simply had to adjust the annual local government settlement. But Thatcher's government wanted to do more. If her "market economics" were to have any chance of success, the socialist corporatism which was embedded in a number of town halls would have to be dislodged. The welfarism associated with large council housing stock were anathema to the Thatcher vision of self-provision.

Two initiatives ensued. The first intervention was to introduce a system of rate capping. This meant that having determined what allowances the central government was going to make the local authority was then given a budget level which it could not exceed. Failure to keep within that predetermined limit would attract a penalty. To stay within the limit invariably meant either a reduction of staff or a reduction in service provision or both. In areas where Black people constituted a measurable proportion of the population they were disproportionately represented in those losing their jobs and in those suffering from reduction of services.

There was a strong correlation between council house tenancy and Labour Party loyalty. Sale of council housing would not only reduce the corporate size of the public sector debt associated with housing but

17

hopefully by cutting the link between council house tenancy and Labour Party loyalty create a bond between the new home owners and their champions, the Tory Party. Indeed some Tory led authorities sought to manipulate the sale of their housing stock in such a way as to create a stable Tory voting majority in some wards.

The sale of council housing had two consequences for a number of Black people. Normally Black people got allocated to the poorer and less desirable estates in the first instance. The best options towards better accommodation very often came through the exercise of a transfer. Since the best buys were obviously on the better estates and first options went to existing tenants. Black people who wanted to exercise the right to buy were often doing so from a less favourable position than white people.

When in 1960 the Greater London Council came into being the Tories had hoped that they had found a way of controlling the political destiny of London. The former London County Council made up of the twelve inner boroughs was a strong labour base. This could surely be diluted by adding all the surrounding suburbs and creating a large Greater London Council which would certainly be consistently Conservative. Repeat this in the other main urban areas and together with the traditional county councils they would have a relatively stable strategic top tier of local government.

Soon, however, things were not looking so certain. By the time Thatcher came to power most of the metropolitan county councils had had or were still under labour control. Over a third of the population in England lived in the metropolitan county council areas and their leaders carried a corresponding political clout. From the balcony of the House of Commons over-looking the Thames, Thatcher could look across the river at the imposing sight of County Hall, seat of the Greater London Council (GLC) and its then leader, Ken Livingstone. He stood for everything Thatcher hated and in an act of sheer political vandalism she determined its demise. But she could not dispose of the GLC without doing the same with the other metropolitan county councils, so they all had to go.

In its pursuit of equal opportunities and in particular its attempts through its purchasing power to use the concept of contract compliance to extend the principles of equal opportunities to its suppliers, the GLC had enraged the National Association of Freedom and its allies who rejoiced at the Thatcher decision.

The other metropolitan county councils led the way, in collaboration with the Greater London Council in the development of equal opportunity policies. (The GLC's first Race Equality Officer, Herman Ouseley later became the first Black Chairman of the Commission for Racial Equality). In addition, they had gone some way in the development of a trained cadre of Black local government officers and in the support of a range of projects managed by the Black communities in the metropolitan areas. The GLC had also been influential in getting the London Fire Brigade to adopt progressive anti-discriminatory practices. It is a matter of record that within 5 years of the demise of the metropolitan county councils 90% of the Black projects that were being assisted by them had lost their public funding with the consequential staff redundancies and loss to the community of vital support services.

The loss of the contract compliance thrust which the GLC and the other metropolitan councils had started to make meant that many suppliers no longer felt any obligation to maintain equal and fair treatment and thus to operate in a level playing field.

Not only did the metropolitan county councils go, but in killing them off, an act now publicly admitted by Lord Howe as a mistake, it was necessary to make the Inner London Education Authority defunct as well. For no educational reason whatsoever, the largest educational authority in Western Europe was to be broken up with all the trauma that entailed. Thatcher who had placed so much store on parental choice failed to listen to the overwhelming majority of parents who wanted the authority retained.

Approximately 20 percent of the Black children of school age in England, Scotland and Wales lived in the Inner London Education Authority's area. Hence the disruption to schooling and the loss of specialist opportunities which the larger authority offered meant that irreparable damage was being done to the educational prospects of many of these young people. A number of the new educational authorities took two years to settle down. In which time we have witnessed an increase in delinquency among Black youngsters beyond the normal expectations. There have been attempts to shift responsibility for this on to the local authorities but the real cause rested in the decision to dismember the ILEA. It will take a decade for the Black community in general to recover from the damage this has caused to the education of their children; but for some particular families the position is irretrievable.

We have seen how the main thrust of Thatcherism was to free the labour market of any constraints that might have been imposed by government. It was argued that this was the most efficient way of improving the Gross National Product (GNP) and that if the GNP was in a healthy state of growth then everybody would share in the wealth that was created. There is no evidence to justify such a claim.

But to achieve her objective Thatcher had to do more than just cap the expenditure of those labour authorities she so delighted in accusing of fiscal mismanagement. Gradually by a series of devices more and

19

more of the real decision making was removed from local authority involvement and taken centrally. For a government that claimed to be promoting and encouraging personal responsibility and individual choice it did more to concentrate power and decision making at the centre in Whitehall than any other European government has done. Simon Jenkins in his book *Accountable to None: The Tory Nationalism of Britain* sets out how while calling themselves decentralisers the Thatcherites set about centralising Britain.

Functions previously overseen by elected people are now controlled by non-elected appointees of government. A transparent system of election has been replaced by a shadowy, potentially corrupt, process of secret appointments, from which large sections of the community are excluded. We have a virtual quango state, with Commissions, Boards, Regulatory Bodies, Training Councils, Trusts, Agencies all appointed by Central Government in a framework where neither they nor the appointing Ministers appear to accept responsibility when anything goes wrong and where neither accepts accountability to the public.

What is of particular concern to the Black community is that they had only just begun to take a really active part in the local political arena with increasing numbers of them being elected as local councillors in those authorities where their communities are concentrated. They have thus come on the stage when less and less influence is left with local authorities than they had previously. Of the approximately 2000 people elected to public office serving London under 10% are from the Black communities. There are approximately 10,000 people appointed to public bodies serving London of whom less than 2% were from the Black communities. In fact although there are fewer elected posts Black people are five times as likely to be elected than they are to be appointed. In addition, the likelihood of being appointed is significantly increased if one is both a Conservative Party member or known sympathiser and business person. Many Black people as a consequence have felt excluded from the Thatcherite experiment.

The assault on local government structures in a concerted strategy of removing political opposition did in fact substantially reduce the involvement and status of Black people in the delivery of services. This had the effect of further undermining their sense of security in the society and reinforced feelings of being undervalued.

THE EFFECTS OF PRIVATISATION
The big debate surrounding the privatisation of public sector industries had been around the perceived greed of the new Boards and Top managements. While the government argued that the real benefits of

privatisation would come through competition, most of the new companies were given time before they would come up against the fierce realities of competition. While preparing for that day, they indulged themselves on the fruits of the monopolies they had obtained to acquire huge rewards for themselves. Through asset stripping, restructuring, down-sizing, delayering and every other devise they sought to make quick profits.

For some it was a licence to print money. Performance related pay was another way of saying the more people you sacked the more you got. Throwing fellow human beings on the scrap heap was carried out with an unashamed zeal. The new companies did not see themselves bound by the commitments of the nationalised Boards to work towards race equality objectives and in the area of job losses Black employees once again got the rough end of the stick.

But Black people lost out in another way as well. As long as the industries remained in public ownership, they like any other citizen had a stake in the asset. Once they were sold at below market value prices, the government pocketed the money not to provide benefits to the whole community but to finance tax cuts and tax breaks largely for their supporters.

Those who could afford to buy shares (i.e. pay money to buy back shares in an industry whose assets they already owned) did so only to discover that the well publicised opportunity to join the shareholder society meant absolutely nothing since small shareholders were at the mercy of the corporate shareholders who were the ones who really ran the new industries. The small shareholders were repeatedly out voted, often by the proxy votes of the corporate shareholders who did not even turn up at the meetings.

Those who could not afford to buy shares, and Black people were disproportionately involved in that grouping were just victims of this "legalised fraud" carried out by a government elected by a system that produced a majority of MPs from a minority of the number of people voting and a still larger minority of the people eligible to vote.

The latest of these privatisations is British Rail. It is important to the Black communities because it and London Transport employed the largest number of Black people within the public sector industries. British Rail has been divided into over 70 companies. If the previous privatisation patterns repeat themselves, then we will be looking at thousands of Black workers being made redundant. A large number of these will be over fifty years old and will face the prospect of not working again in Britain. This is the big one as far as the Black community is concerned. What happens here will determine how easy it will be for the Black communities to find a way back from the tragedy that the Thatcher years have bequeathed to them.

21

THE PRINCE AND THATCHER

Addressing a conference on the 11th March 1996 in Manchester to relaunch his charities, bringing them under one umbrella to be known as the Prince's Trust, Prince Charles said that unemployment, drug abuse, homelessness and academic under achievement had resulted in hundreds of thousands of young people not playing their full part as citizens.

The Prince told staff and volunteers at the launch that:

"We will never realise our full economic potential in this country until standards of education and training match those of our competitors... We will never regenerate our inner cities until young people care about their communities and have a greater sense of citizenship."

The Prince's Trust is Britain's major charity working with young people. Through its activity in the inner city and with young entrepreneurs it has given new hope to many Black young people, who have found the charity more approachable than other agencies.

The Prince is a firm believer in partnership between the various sectors that make up the life of our nation. In his interview with Jonathan Dimbleby he declared that he would hope he could be considered as "defender of faiths." It is this sense of inclusiveness that is so important.

Throughout the 1980s the Prince has developed a deep conviction that Government's enabling role went beyond the financing of research and development to the laying down of environmental standards. He could therefore be viewed as a moderate interventionist.

This was certainly not Thatcher's most likely style. Through the Prince's Trust he had been working in the inner city and with ethnic minorities. When Thatcher declared following her 1987 victory that one of her priorities was to tackle the problems of the inner cities, he grasped the opportunity and suggested to her that she should go into the inner city herself and meet some of those who were actually doing work in their communities in the inner city. He told her that he honestly believed that if she met them, they would tell her what the problems were and what was required. He offered to lay on a lunch at Kensington Palace to facilitate the meeting.

She did not accept at first and it was a year later before he got her to agree to invite these inner city activists to No. 10 for lunch. The plans were however dropped and it was some time before he got matters reviewed. The Prince advised the invited community entrepreneurs that they should avoid making political points or getting at her and scoring points. The meeting lasted three hours in the Cabinet room. One of the

Black people who was present said that while nothing appeared to happen immediately, slowly little initiatives started to come out from different departments which closely resembled some of the discussion that had gone on in the Cabinet room that day. He was full of praise for the Prince in sticking to it and getting them that hearing with the Prime Minister.

THE JUDGEMENT
It may be too early for a final judgement on the Thatcher years, but even some of her staunchest followers are beginning to come to grips with the meaning of her crusade. Alan Howarth the MP for Stratford-upon-Avon justifying his move from the Conservative Party to the Labour Party on the eve of the Conservative party conference in 1995 had this to say:

"I responded to Margaret Thatcher's project because of her challenge to inherited orthodoxies and the establishment, her courage and her moral energy. Thatcher's fervour proved, however, to lack generosity. Her crusade to cast off the shackles of big government became a license for Darwinian individualism. Her radicalism hardened into an intolerant new orthodoxy. Her heirs practice either a listless pastiche of Thatcherism or a ferocious caricature of it."[4]

Tony Blair explaining how the Easter story had helped to shape his political outlook referred to the controversy caused by Margaret Thatcher when she quoted St Paul's letter to the Thessolonians, "If a man will not work, he shall not eat." He commented:

"This injunction by Paul should never be used to justify the withdrawal of support from the helpless."[5]

23

Ethnic minority
participation in the
world of work and
business

"I had found something to do with my life that was honourable and useful, that I could do well, and that I loved doing. That is a rare good fortune in anyone's life. My only regret was that I could not do it all over again."

Colin Powell - *My American Journey*,
Random House, New York 1995

CHAPTER TWO

FREE MARKET OR SLAVE LABOUR

MINIMUM WAGE

The Major Government secured an opt out from the Maastricht Treaty from the Social Chapter. This has been labelled by the Tory Party, the National Association for Freedom and others as a great triumph. Labour while asserting that it is fully committed to the Social Chapter has as recently as its 1995 Party conference failed to go beyond saying that it would institute a minimum wage without indicating what level that should be.

This debate is of extreme importance to Black workers who still constitute a disproportionate number of the unskilled labour force. Look around and anywhere you see a disproportionate number of Black people at work you can rest assured the pay is low. The free market proponents argue that labour is just another commodity to be bought and sold on the market, its price being determined by the law of supply and demand. But as long ago as Pope Leo XIII's Encyclical repeated by successive Popes, the Christian Socialist position is that a workman who "through necessity or fear of a worse evil" accepts unduly harsh conditions of work "is made the victim of force and injustice."

The state in a civilised society has an unmistakable obligation to ensure that the conditions of work do not undermine human dignity. Attempting to pay sweat shop wages in Britain does just that and it is immoral and unjust. So when the government argues that wage levels are partly and solely a matter for the individual and the employer they are propounding an unsustainable argument. Contracts are not truly "free" when the process is conducted in an environment of unregulated economic necessity by grossly unequal parties. Workers should not be forced by the prospect of the dole or destitution through the withdrawal of the dole, to sell their labour for an unjust wage, or to work under inhuman conditions.

But that is precisely what many Black workers face if the government continues with its programme of deregulation. Unconstrained capitalism may in the short term increase the wealth of the few, but it is no more than a recipe for slave labour and in the long term social incohesion.

So far the cumulative effect of the government's initiatives in deregulation has been to create intense uncertainty as managements taking a hint from government have become more and more inconsiderate in their dealings with their work forces. In their rush to increase profits there has been a tendency to move roughshod over the labour force. The weaker groups with little political or collective clout have tended to suffer the greater.

Sir James Goldsmith, the billionaire MEP, who has come upon the British scene with the launch of the new Referendum Party is no particular friend of the British working class but even he recognises the damage being done to British prestige abroad. He scoffs: "They are selling Britain as the Mexico of Europe, as if it was an honour to pay low wages. We've gone mad." In his tract, "The Trap" which he published three years ago, he set out a view of the free market to which the present Major government is so committed by saying:

"Global free trade will shatter the way in which value-added is shared between capital and labour... In mature societies, we have been able to level up a general agreement as to how it should be shared."[1]

In what could be a direct slur on Third World labour in the European context he adds:

"Oversight that agreement will be destroyed by the arrival of huge populations willing to undercut radically the salaries earned by our workforces. The social divisions that this will cause will be deeper than anything even envisaged by Marx."[2]

But politicians who should be equally concerned with improving living standards as with social cohesion now find themselves captives of the big multi nationals, their bankers and brokers who manipulate asset control according to a code of profit maximisation for protected interest groups whatever the impact on labour markets and the consequential social impacts. Governments are more concerned about the impact of their decisions on the whims of the money market than they are about the likelihood of their citizens. The tragedy is that they try to convince us that the two are the same.

The government continues to cite UK wage structure and minimal employee protection as the reasons for improved inward investment. Whether that is true or not, the reality is that the bulk of the inward investment has gone to areas of low ethnic minority concentration and has been of little benefit to Black workers.

BLACK INVOLVEMENT IN THE LABOUR FORCE

There has been a remarkable shift in the working patterns of Black people over the last twenty years. In 1972 extracts from the General Household Survey revealed that 91% of ethnic minority men compared with 77% of White men "were working". But by the Spring of 1995 the number of ethnic minority men had dropped to 60%. But they were unevenly distributed. Among Black men we had 57% at work, among Indians 72% and among Pakistani/Bangledeshi some 49%. The number of White men at work stood at 77%.

TABLE 1. Economic status of people of working Age: by gender and ethnic group - Spring 1995

	White	Black	Indian	Pakistani Bangladeshi	Other	All Ethnic Group
MALE						
Working Full-Time	72	49	65	41	51	71
Working Part-Time	5	8	7	8	8	5
Unemployed	8	21	10	18	12	9
Inactive	15	22	18	33	29	15
All (Thousand)	16,933	273	306	216	224	18,017
FEMALE						
Working Full-Time	38	37	36	12	30	38
Working Part-Time	24	15	19	6	16	28
Unemployed	5	14	7	7	8	5
Inactive	28	34	38	75	46	29
All (Thousand)	15,420	296	279	191	238	16,428

Source: Labour Force Survey - Central Statistical Office

Overall 44% of ethnic minority women compared with 62% of White women are at work. Again the distribution is varied. 52% among Black women 55% among Indians and 18% among Pakistani and Bangladeshi women. This reflects the continuing difference between Muslim and non-Muslim women. It also illustrates while the position of Muslim women in the labour force remains much at it was in the early 70s that of non-Muslin women has grown to the point where it now out-strips that of Black women.

It is also important to note that while 77% White males compared to 66% of White females are working, the relative figures among the ethnic minority groups are Black 57% male 52% female; Indian 72% male 55% female, and Pakistani/Bangladeshi 49% male, 18% female. It has already been pointed out how the Muslim cultural position affects the role of women in regard to labour force activity. It should also be noted that the closeness in the proportion of Black women working may be linked to the number of them who are heads of households as single parents.

1 in 15 White men are working part-time. 1 in 7 Black men. 1 in 10 Indian men and 1 in 6 Pakistani/Bangladeshi men. For all groups the situation is much worse for women. It is 3 in 7 White women, 3 in 10 Black women 4 in 11 Indian and 1 in 3 Pakistani. Because most of the part-time work is low pay work with little security and poor benefits, there is scope for continued social tensions. The high levels of unemployment, and economic inactivity represent a colossal waste of talent. Far from what is generally propulgated about the abilities of Black people the 1996 Social Trend Survey has a very interesting statement to make:

"Although in general, a higher proportion of men than women have a qualification, the gap is smallest among those of Black ethnic origin and largest among those from the Pakistani/Bangladeshi ethnic group. Both men and women from the Black ethnic group are more likely than those of White ethnic origin to have a qualification, although this difference may be a reflection of the younger age structures of the Black population."

While the job levels of Asian and West Indian men remain substantially lower than those of white men, the gap between Pakistani/Bangladeshi men is still the widest followed by West Indians. Indians have made the greatest advance but have not closed the gap. If they maintain the current rate over the next two decades they should, like the Jews, have made themselves economically secure. That does not imply that discrimination against them would have ended but that they would have carved out a position in the labour market from which to ensure that their interests are safeguarded.

One issue compounding the adverse labour market position of Black people is their age profile. While just around 20% of the White population is under 16 years of age the corresponding figure for the Black community is around 30%, with figures of 29% among African/West Indian people, 25% among Indians and 40.6% among Pakistani and Bangladeshi according to the Spring 1995 Labour Force survey. It will take at least another generation or two to even out this profile and bring the White and non-White under 16s into some sort of parity. The result being that they will continue to be disproportionately affected by the high levels of youth unemployment which has struck the country since the early 80s.

TABLE 2. Population by ethnic group and age. Spring 1995

	Under 16	16-29	30-44	45-59	60+	All Ages (Thousand)
Ethnic Minority Group						
Black[1]	29.0	25.5	27.0	11.3	7.2	869
Indian	25.0	26.0	25.5	16.0	7.5	844
Pakistani/Bangladeshi	40.6	26.4	10.4	9.3	4.3	725
Other[2]	37.2	23.3	26.0	9.6	3.9	733
All Minority Groups	32.6	25.3	24.6	11.7	5.8	32.11
White	20.1	19.0	21.6	18.3	20.9	52.844
All Ethnic Groups[3]	209	19.4	21.8	18.0	20.1	56.1231

1. Includes Caribbean, African and other Black people of non-mixed origin.
2. Includes Chinese, other ethnic minority groups of non-mixed origin and those of mixed origin
3. Includes ethnic groups not stated.

Source: Labour Force Survey. Central Statistical Office

A second factor influencing the position of Black people in the labour market is their concentration in inner city areas which are the areas of highest unemployment. This has not been helped by the Thatcherite struggle with the unions which was fought on the principle of high unemployment. Scarcely had that ended than the economy was overtaken by a sustained recession. During this period the manufacturing industry was on the one hand engaged in flight from the inner city and on the other closures through business failure, mergers and rationalization.

The fast growing industries of Banking, Finance, Insurance and

29

Computing are not as yet taking their fair share of Black employees. They employ 8.6% of the White population but only 6.3% of the Black population, and as we have seen qualifications cannot provide the alibi since Black workers are by and large better qualified than White workers. The 1985 Labour Force Survey revealed that while 13.4% of White men had a higher qualification, the equivalent for non-White men was 18.3%.

TABLE 3. Unemployment Rates by Ethnic Group. Spring 1994

	Long Term	Total Unemployment
White	4.00	9.1
Black	15.8	26.2
Indian	8.0	14.0
Pakistani/Banglesdeshi	15.0	27.9

Source: Employment Department

The Pakistani and Bangledeshi ethnic groups have the highest level of unemployment but are closely followed by the African and Caribbean groups - 27.9% to 26.2%. Their unemployment level is twice as great as the Indian level and three times as great as the White group. When we analyse the long term employment as a proportion of the total unemployment in each group we find that among African and Caribbean groups long term unemployment constitutes 60% of their unemployment. The percentage for Indian, Pakistani/Bangladeshi and White are respectively 57%, 54%, and 44%. These national averages will be substantially increased in the inner cities where unemployment levels are the highest.

RACIAL DISCRIMINATION IN EMPLOYMENT
Racial discrimination is still rampant at every level of the employment stage. After 30 years of race relations legislation we are facing some of the same old attitudes. The Commission for Racial Equality (CRE) continues its two pronged assault on discrimination in the work place. It endeavours to promote good practise through liaison with businesses as trades unions and professional bodies as one part of the strategy. The other is to use its quasi-judical powers to conduct investigations where it believes malpractices are taking place and to assist complainants who are seeking redress against acts of discrimination.

The CRE received 547 employment complaints in 1981. These had risen to 619 by 1986. In 1991 they had 1203 a slight drop in 1993 to 1160 and back up to 1300 in 1995. There has been steady growth. But not all complaints are processed through the CRE about as many again go direct to the Industrial Tribunal. Many more potential cases are never raised because the victims feel cornered in the situation and are unable to cope with the stress and uncertainty involved. The CRE figures therefore represent only the tip of the iceberg.

One vital change in the law which is urgently needed is the introduction of class actions. As the law currently stands each individual must institute his/her proceedings and go through the full process. In the United States where several individuals are suffering the same discrimination from the same employer, it is only necessary to prove a test case and apply those results to all other persons in the same category or class. Such a change would considerably enhance the law.

Commenting on the absence of Black faces on the floor of the Stock Exchange, Angus Phaure, a member of the Stock Exchange and a director of County Securities wrote in the letters column of the Financial Times as follows:

"The absence of Black faces from the floor of the House is a matter of serious concern. We need to make sure that everyone who lives in Britain identifies with and feels a part of its society.... City recruiters say that people in the Stock Exchange wouldn't like working with Blacks, and therefore it is better to choose White candidates. This is not true, however, and once you are in, there is absolutely no discrimination"[3]

But the majority of the few who do get in do not share his optimism. Although new technology has forced a number of changes in the city reducing the dependency on the Old Boy Network it has not killed it off. As long as that network survives, discrimination against Black people will be a natural and inevitable corollary. But it is not only the City. Wherever in the Establishment the Old Boy Network flourishes Black people have found the route to entrance barred by discrimination.

Out of Court settlements are a favourite device of large organisations. They will often let the issue run and run so as to wear down the victim. Then either shortly before the hearing or half way through the hearing they will come up with an offer, accompanied by a gagging clause forbidding the victim to talk about terms of the settlement and allowing the organisation to avoid having a judgement against them.

Former model Jacqueline Oliver found herself in one such situation. She was a perfume saleswoman for the French firm Givenchy at their Harvey Nichols store in Knightbridge. She had been told she would have to work harder because of her colour, and had been subjected to months of racial harassment by her line manager. Despite that she had won a national award for selling more of the firm's products than any other sales assistant. The firm moved her to Debenham in Oxford Street.

She complained to the CRE and gained their assistance. Givenchy claimed that they had made the move because Harvey Nichols had asked them to remove Miss Oliver. The basis of the request was poor timekeeping, untidy appearance of her counter and her constant use of the telephone. Harvey Nichols denied making any such request.

Givenchy had dismissed her after she had complained to the CRE, a further breach of the Race Relations Act 1976, since she was being victimised for exercising her legitimate right. Three days into the hearing Givenchy initiated negotiations with Miss Oliver and after some five hours arrived at an out of court settlement.

Following a two year investigation the CRE has established levels of racial discrimination in the Armed Services and the Ministry of Defence has undertaken to institute measures to put things right. This should hopefully open the door for many more Black people to join the armed forces. It is worthy to note that a Black man in the person of Colin Powell, rose through the ranks to become a four star General, Chairman of the US Armed Forces Joint Chief of Staff, National Security Advisor. He master minded the UN forces including UK forces, Desert Storm in Kuwait. In Britain, Black men and women are having difficulty getting into the Armed Forces. It is not any part of the argument that the US is free of racial discrimination, but rather; that there are mechanisms that facilitate those who would grasp the hand of opportunity.

Reflecting on his life, Colin Powell said:

"If Luther and Arne (his father and mother) had shipped out for Southampton instead of New York City, I might have made sergeant major in a modest British regiment, but not likely British Chief of Staff. I treasure my family's British roots, but I love our America, land of opportunity."[4]

There is no area of employment in which racial discrimination does not exist. In the now fashionable exercises of restructuring, downsizing, delayering and outsourcing all strategies for reducing staff organisation have paid little attention to ensure that principles of equal opportunity are preserved. In these exercises Black staff are more likely to be made redundant than their White counterparts and where they are retained they are less likely than their White colleagues to retain jobs of equivalent status. This is certainly an area that would profit from a formal investigation by the Commission for Racial Equality.

The CRE conducted a survey of the large companies in Britain in 1994. These were companies who employed more than 7000 people in the U.K. Out of the 168 companies, 147 reported that they had policies covering racial equality and the CRE noted that the larger the company, the more likely it was to have a policy.[5]

The statutory Race Relations Code of Practice in Employment came into effect in 1984 and this has been a pivotal date ever since. 42 of the companies had policies in place before 1984; 67 introduced policies between 1984 and 1989 and 38 had developed their policies between 1989 and 1994. In the decade since the introduction of the Code of Practice some 105 companies had developed policies covering racial equality.

51% of the companies had regular ethnic monitoring as an element in their racial equality programmes. 49% included racial equality training, 46% had racial harassment procedures, only 8% raised racial equality issues with their subcontractors. When one examined what was being monitored, the CRE found that 40% monitored for the total workforce, 31% by department, 36% by grade, 31% by job application but only 10% by application for promotion, 5% by training course participation, 5% by appraisal and 4% by those made redundant. The failure by the vast majority of firms to monitor promotion, appraisal and training opportunities is worrying to say the least.

What the survey emphasized was the fact that the development of policy is only the start of the process. Planning effective programmes of implementation can be harder. The baseline is not whether you have recruited the odd Black person here or there, but whether having recruited them they are able to access all the facilities of the company and to make as full a contribution to the company's success as their talents would allow.

The CRE has produced a handbook for employers to assist them in systematically working towards excellence in the implementation of their racial equality policies. It is called "Racial Equality Means Business. A standard for racial equality for Employers." It sets out some six key result areas - Policy and Planning, Selecting, Developing and Retaining Staff, Communication and Corporate Image, Corporate Citizenship and Auditing for Racial Equality. Each area has five performance levels with level five representing the equality standard.

Most companies are now engaged in some form of quality control. It is important to recognise that the goal of total quality assurance cannot be achieved without having met the equality standards.

A survey commissioned by the Employment Service in 1992 and conducted by Public Attitude Surveys Limited revealed that "38% of all non-White respondents agreed that those from ethnic minorities are treated worse by employers than are White individuals and 36% felt they had been unfairly treated by employers in the past five years due to their ethnic origin. This proportion rose to 49% in the case of Black

33

African respondents and was still over one in four (28%) for the Bangladeshi/Pakistani group."[6]

The major complaint against employers was that the discrimination was present from the onset of the search for a job. Some 45% of those who felt badly treated supported that claim. The other issues raised and the variance between the different groups are set out in the table below:

TABLE 4. Nature or discrimination by employers - all respondents feeling unfairly treated by employers.[7]

	Ethnic Group			
	Non-White total (436) %	Indian (8%) %	Bangadeshi Pakistani (66) %	Black Caribbean (113) %
1. When applying for job, sees name/colour	45	37	56	43
2. Assumed that spoken English is poor	16	14	17	23
3. Accused of poor work/ not working had enough	13	14	5	17
4. Thought bad for service to employ ethnic minority	10	12	8	12
5. No real proof just a feeling/ atmosphere	7	4	6	4
6. Abuse/racial name calling	4	5	5	5
7. Employer not as friendly treats me differently	4	7	3	3

Source: Public Attitude Survey Ltd.

As if these difficulties being faced by Black people seeking employment were not great enough, the government is seeking to add another. The government is concerned that the number of persons who are working illegally is growing, and in order to stem the tide as they see it, they have drawn up proposals to place a duty on employers to ensure that those people whom they employ are legally entitled to work in this country. This in effect means working as unpaid immigration officers.

Employers believe that the process of checking eligibility could be complicated and onerous. With the threat of prosecution hanging over their heads together with heavy fines many will be tempted to take the easy way out by finding reasons not to employ Black people who seek employment. Some will doubtless be genuinely glad for the alibi others will succumb to a legitimate fear. The government has so far shown no signs of shifting its ground.

Speaking in the House of Lords in October 1994, Home Office Minister Baroness Blatch confirmed that Britain would not ratify the 1983 European Convention on the legal statues of Migrant Workers as it went beyond the existing international commitment on access to labour markets and would be incompatible in several respects with the provisions of the immigration rules.

When one considers that access to employment is pivoted to access to proper housing and choice of where that housing happens to be and the impact that has on educational opportunity for one's family, it is clear to see how the discrimination experienced in the search for employment affects the total life experience of Black families.

TRADES UNION MOVEMENT AND RACE
The Trades Union Congress Black Workers Charter offered advice to its affiliate unions in these terms: "It is no good trades unions only talking about equal opportunities; talk has to be translated into action. To show that they are truly committed to equal opportunities for Black workers, trades unions can, and should, examine their own structures and organisation." Most of the larger unions had already been pursuing race equality procedures and structures. The Transport and General Workers Union and Unison, are two of the unions with the most developed policies. Over the last five years, the unions have been paying greater attention to the needs of their Black members as a direct result of their response to the TUC Black Workers Charter initiatives.

The TUC Race Relations Advisory Committee has sought to influence the work of its affiliates and raise the profile of Black workers through the sponsoring of National Conferences, but there are still too few Black people at the Annual TUC conference. Bill Morris, the most senior Black Trades Unionist not only in Britain but in Western Europe must not be left alone in the higher reaches of the Trades Union movement. Other Black Trades Unionists must be identified and trained for office.

The TUC with the help of the CRE has provided guidance to its affiliates on monitoring union membership and on the handling of race related grievances. The experience of many Black workers had been that when it came to getting full backing from the largely white union hierarchy in the pursuit of their grievances they were faced with less than wholehearted support. Many representatives felt unsure of their grounds when dealing with grievances in which race was an issue. The complainant's perception of what constituted an issue of race and that of the representative often differed. The respondent, indeed, had another and still more removed perception.

A similar situation arose over representation in disciplinaries. In some work environments some Black workers tried to convert every situation into a racially motivated incident. This has tended to immobilise some representatives. It is an area in which much more training is required.

The TUC has also issued guidance and run seminars on racial discrimination and harassment in the work-place. The TGWU negotiators' guide carried the stern reminder:

"Remember, the failure of a union to act at all in a race relations case can bring it into the Tribunal as a defendant - a discouraging sight for potential Black recruits and all members keen to tackle racism"[8]

Many Unions now negotiate equal opportunity policies as part of their regular consultation and negotiating procedures. The principal areas involved are recruitment, selection and promotion, extended leave; racial harassment, ethnic monitoring. As the confidence of union negotiators grows and as the employers come to accept the business sense underpinning equal opportunity they are extending into more and more areas.

The vast majority of unionised Black workers are covered by some form of race equality policy. While these policies may not be perfect, at least they constitute a framework and a firm beginning upon which to build. The difficulty remains with the growing number of Black workers outside the union umbrella working in de-regulated environments.

BUSINESS ENTERPRISES
One answer to the complex of disadvantage and discrimination has been to take the route of self employment. Some 23% of Asian men are self-employed or running their own small businesses and employing others. This compares with 14% of White men and 8.5% of West Indian men.

By and large the majority of the Asian businesses are run by those of Indian origin with the majority of those having arrived in Britain from East Africa in the late 60s and early 70s. They have made substantial progress in building an economic base from which to approach the 21st century. There are just under 5000 Asian restaurants with a business value of around £6 billion. The value of their retail interest is not known but in terms of interest held by other ethnic minority settler groups it is second only to the Jewish interests.

Had it not been for the collapse of BCCI which caused a bit of a hiccup in the expansion drive, the market share of Asian businesses in the UK would have been much healthier. By sheer hardwork, family support and community underpinning - certainly without as much help from the commercial banks as they might have expected - they have converted the corner shop image of the 60s to main players as we approach the end of the century.

Very few of the African Caribbean immigrants had been engaged in business before coming to Britain and so the early businesses were geared to supplying services to the community which did not involve much capital outlay. They have not made the same effort to commercialise their foods. There are probably less than 100 African Caribbean restaurants in Britain. Most of the up and coming businesses are run by people under 35 and mostly women highly educated and generally with some form of business training. There is still considerable reticence by banks in supporting Black entrepreneurs. Banks have not been particularly helpful to small businesses in general so it is not surprising that Black small businesses have particular problems. This is as much a reflection of the times as it is evidence of the level of discrimination.

Investing in our
multicultural future
through education

> "The demand for recognition, animated by the ideal of human dignity points in at least two directions, both to the protection of the basic rights of individuals as human beings and to the acknowledgement of the particular needs of individuals as members of specific cultural groups."

Amy Gutman
Director, University Centre for Human Values

CHAPTER THREE

THE EDUCATIONAL CHALLENGE

THE NATIONAL CURRICULUM

Midway through their second term of office, the Thatcher Government started to lay the foundations for a National Curriculum. Having decided on breaking the control local government (largely Labour) had on education they decided on allowing schools to cut free of local control. But to make that acceptable, two other mechanisms were necessary. The first was to devise a National Curriculum which all schools should follow and a system for testing the performance of schools in relation to the National Curriculum. The second was to revise the inspectorate into an agency one step removed from the Department of Education and Science.

There was no problem as far as the Three R's were concerned. Employers had long been complaining that by far too many children were leaving school without having the tools of numeracy and literacy to enable them to be useful employees. Additional concerns however to the Black community were the place in the curriculum for recognition of religions other than Christianity, a version of history other than the Anglo-Saxon view of the imperial past and a place for non-European languages in preparation for a wider involvement with the emerging markets of the developing countries of Africa and Asia.

MULTICULTURAL EDUCATION

The Swann Report of 1985 is the most recent case advanced for the development of a coherent multicultural education system in order to provide an education for all children which would assist them in meeting the challenge of modern society. It resulted from an inquiry into the Education of Children from Ethnic Minority Groups which was chaired by Lord Swann. The report title was "Education for All."

Swann saw the enhancement of multicultural education as providing all children with a broader and richer understanding of the world around them. However Simon Pearce argues that this was not to be achieved through what Matthew Arnold would have called the embracing of "the best that has been thought and known in the world."[1] It would use education "not as a means of seeking and transmitting truth," but "rather as an engine of social change".[2] He further contends that it was to be implemented by the subordination of education to political ends regardless of the educational consequences.[3]

Swann indeed calls for the need to re-examine the basic ethnocentric nature of education to see whether it fully meets today's needs. Swann unlike what many of his critics contend, does not seek the ending of the British culture, but rather urges the humility to accept that while it remains the largest cultural influence in the society, there are other cultures and values which require recognition and acknowledgement. Indeed minority cultures will never be able to fully contribute to the national whole until they are afforded that recognition.

It is a prerequisite to social cohesion and a necessary value to be included into all parts of the educational system. But the objectives must be clear and the approach compatible with the search for truth and mindful of the relative reality which experiences have helped to frame for each individual's set of values. Formal education systems are not the sole, and may not even be the prime drive behind the development of the full appreciation of multiculturalism, but they have an important role to play which must not be underrated.

Education ought to provide us with the tools with which both to examine and to appreciate the world around us in all its rich diversity. It is this very challenging exploration that is at the heart of multiculturalism. What it says is this. Here we are, a diverse people drawn from different lands with different religions and cultural values, but contributing to a new national experience determined to help each other have a full life experience while sharing together in the building of a better society.

Despite its detractors some geninue progress has been made towards achieving many of these goals. But while recognising those gains it is important to recognise that considerable levels of racism still exist within the system and that is bound to affect the smooth progress towards a fully multicultural society.

40

While the most prevalent form of racism confronting British society is that of white racism it must be borne in mind that different individuals and groups respond differently based on their own inner resources and tolerance levels. It is no defence against the indictment of racism to assert that some ethnic minority groups are doing better than others. This is but a natural expectation, what we need to understand is what contributes to that difference in response.

The opponents of multi-culturalism are the same little Englanders who having joined the European Union now bleat about loss of sovereignty and rule from Brussels. They claim that the promotion of multiculturalism will mean the reappraisal of British history, their political institutions and every other value they have ever held dear. In a sort of frenzied hysteria they reject the concept of a "pluralist" society as being the invention of a liberal propogandist lobby bent on depriving the British people of their culture and historic place in life. They have seized on every mistake made by the anti-racist lobby to feed the fears of people left insecure by their loss of power and status in the world.

So paranoid are they about Islam, that even those who have long forsaken any allegiance to Christianity recoil at the concept of a multi-faith religious education commitment as a threat to Christian values. And yet if we are to achieve a genuinely pluralistic multicultural society, then respect for and understanding of religious difference is an imperative.

THE LANGUAGE OF LEAGUE TABLES

Having introduced a series of national tests to back up the National Curriculum the government decided on publicising the results in the form of league tables. The rationale was that by so doing valuable information was being passed on to parents who could use the information to influence the choice of school for their children. The problem with the crude tables so far produced is that they have told us how well particular schools have done with particular sets of examinations. They have told us nothing about a school's ability to improve the performance of its children.

Education is essentially of added value. You take a set of pupils or students and you move them along. It is about extending horizons. If your school is in a favourable environment blessed with good teachers and above average resources both human and material to work with, there ought not to be any surprise that you come amongst the top grouping as a result. Nor indeed should there be any laurels for so doing.

For many Black parents the option of sending their children to other schools just does not exist. Telling them that they are locked into sending their children to schools that are poorly resourced and where the teachers are demoralised, and the buildings inadequate only increases their sense of utter frustration. League tables without genuine opportunity for universal parental choice is nothing short of a national sham. Not even all middle-class people who are the most politically active group in society can exercise the options the league tables are supposed to trigger.

SOME AREAS OF ACHIEVEMENT

Not-with-standing, there have been a number of achievements which need to be recorded since they point to some of the possible ways forward. In February 1996 Christopher Woodhead, the Chief Inspector of Schools, said that children of parents who had emigrated from Africa, Asia and the Caribbean were doing better than local white children in inner city schools. He noted that African and Asian children were doing better than African-Caribbean children. He also nailed the lie that Black children were responsible for the poor performance of inner-city schools.

But the question is not, nor should it be, whether they outperform poor working class white children who have lost the will to benefit from education. It should in fact be whether or not they have developed to their full potential. The apparent achievement may signal that White children particularly White boys may be falling through the net at an accelerated rate. It is equally true that the position of African-Caribbeans has been sustained by their girls rather than their boys. The Thatcher years did greater damage to the psyche of the White working class than it did to Black people and this has run over in the performance of their children at school.

Black parents in general and the aspiring middle classes among them in particular still believe that the only escape route to that better life is through hardwork and qualifications. They will make any sacrifice necessary to see their children achieve. They encourage their offspring to place a premium on self improvement. Where clusters of such families are found in working class areas with their children attending schools with a preponderance of disadvantaged White children it is not surprising that they will out-perform them. This is not an attempt to belittle the achievement, but to put out a flag of caution on factors that need to be taken into account in assessing the value of the statistics.

The greatest successes are achieved where teaching methods match the children's experience and needs. Sudbourne Primary School in Brixton, with a 65 per cent Black ethnic minority pupil roll and where 20% of its pupils speak English as a second language has exceeded the Government set norms for numeracy and literacy for both seven and 11-year olds.

42

TABLE 5. Percentage of Children meeting Government set norms 1995

	Literacy		Numeracy	
	National Average	Sudbourne Performance	National Average	Sudbourne Performance
7 year olds	75	85	75	85+
11 year olds	50	64	50	86+

Here was a clear example of how a school can rise above social deprivation, and the challenges of linguistic difference and variance with a dedicated staff committed to old fashioned attitudes and teaching methods; coupled with a belief in the children's ability to succeed. Headteacher Susan Scarsbrook is not ashamed to admit that teachers at Sudbourne set weekly spelling tests and that pupils actually recite their times-tables. Nor does she hide the fact that the pupils are expected to take books home to read to their parents. They are also expected to practise their spelling at home. This home work brings the parents into partnership with their children's learning.

Brighter children are given harder work to do which allows them to be stretched while the less able children are given more individual attention during twice weekly sessions when the children are banded into ability groups, but generally the programme is based on whole-class teaching. A network of monitors among the older children helped to develop a sense of responsibility and pride.[4]

What Sudbourne has demonstrated is that it is possible to succeed given the right environment and that to a large extent that environment is shaped by the teachers involved. One is reminded of Mahatma Gandhi's statement "It is better to light a candle than to curse the darkness." Hundreds of teachers every school day are lighting candles while thousands are cursing the darkness of deprivation, disadvantage and discrimination. We must continue to search for ways of redressing that imbalance.

Another area of slow but gradual achievement is the number of Black teachers appearing in classrooms and the increasing numbers of them acquiring senior posts. There is still a long way to go before the position reaches a satisfactory level, but it is important to note the steady progress. It is equally important to recognise that the barriers that had to be overcome to make this limited progress are still around.

Throughout the late 1980s a process of ethnic monitoring of teachers was developed both at local authority level and centrally by the Department of Education and Science. In 1989 the Commission for Racial Equality issued a Code of Practice for the elimination of racial discrimination in education. The code demonstrated how the Race Relations Act 1976 would apply to various functions in the educational process and what would constitute unlawful racial discrimination. It covered activity at all levels of the education system from pre-school to university and from students to governing bodies.

As late as 1989, just before the issuing of the Code of practice, a survey of equal opportunities in Higher Education revealed that Universities and Polytechnics (they are all universities now) had not paid much attention to the issues of racial equality and had not recognised any need for the development of specific anti-discriminatory policies. The early 1990s have seen them take their first tentative steps in this area.

Apart from the problems faced by Black teachers in getting appointments in the first place, there are two other common problems to be confronted. One survey conducted by the Commission for Racial Equality[5] revealed that "78 per cent of ethnic minority teachers were on scales 1 or 2 compared with 57 per cent of White teachers." When they looked at the other end of the scales they discovered five per cent of ethnic minority teachers were employed in deputy head or headteacher posts compared with 13 per cent of White teachers. There was also another very intriguing revelation. Ethnic minority male and White female teachers were fairly similarly distributed at both the top end and lower end of the scales and that the ethnic minority female teachers had the worst grade distribution suggesting the highest level of discrimination, probably derived from institutionalised race and sex discrimination.

TABLE 6. Scales of Teachers

	Total	M	F	Total	M	F
Basic: All Teachers	431	192	239	19285	7657	1137
	%	%	%	%	%	%
Scale 1	37	35	38	27	15	36
Scale 2	41	35	46	30	23	35
Scale 3	13	15	11	19	25	15
Scale 4	3	6	1	7	13	3
Senior Teacher	-	1	-	2	3	1
Deputy Head	2	3	1	7	10	5
Head Teachers	3	5	1	6	10	3
DK/NA	1	1	2	7	1	2

Source: CRE Ethnic Minority School Teachers 1988

Further analysis of the data in the CRE survey revealed that it was more likely for ethnic minority teachers in secondary schools to be on lower scales than their White counterparts than it would be for those working in primary schools. The vast majority of ethnic minority teachers (some 98 per cent) taught in schools which did not have any religious affiliation. Of the ethnic minority teachers teaching in secondary schools nearly half (47 per cent) teach mathematics and science. This is a known area of shortage of White teachers.

As more and more responsibility is being passed down to school governors, the greater is the need to ensure that Black ethnic minority groups find ways of improving their representation on school and college governing bodies. It has already been demonstrated that where Black people are taking an active part on the governing boards of schools, those schools are likely to have Black teachers. This does not necessitate their being on the selection panels. Indeed their presence on selection panels should follow appropriate training and experience in common with all other selectors. The current demands on school governors are such that would be governors should undergo preparatory training before putting themselves forward.

Where ethnic minority school governors exist, they are more likely to be of Indian or Caribbean origin than Pakistani or African origin. Fuller ethnic monitoring would be able to identify more readily the trends and the possibilities in this area and help those groups which are lagging behind to develop remedial strategies. But as more schools leave local authority control, the responsibility for ensuring that equal opportunities issues are retained will fall entirely on the governing bodies of the schools and they may be less conscientious in maintaining appropriate equal opportunity systems.

It is perhaps interesting to note that it is more likely to find ethnic minority governors in secondary schools rather than in primary schools. No research evidence exists which might cast any light on the underlying reasons for this trend, but it may reflect a perception of the importance of secondary school governorships or on the process of selection. Whatever the reason, however, efforts should be made to increase the number of ethnic minority governors in primary schools.

RACIAL HARASSMENT
The 90s have witnessed an increase in racial harassment and violence. This has generated a public debate and while Parliament rejected an attempt to get a new specific offence of racial violence it did condemn the scope of racial harassment in 1994. It is unfortunate that the new wave of racial harassment and violence has entered both schools and colleges. The Commission for Racial Equality found it necessary to provide advice for the Committee of Vice-Chancellors and Principals

on the guidance document they were preparing on combating racial harassment in higher education.

Local Education authorities have for some time been producing clear policy guidelines on racial harassment. Because of Section 71 of the Race Relations Act 1976, local authorities were aware of the fact that failure on their part to act on complaints of racial harassment could leave them exposed to being accused of unlawful racial discrimination.

But the focus of racial harassment and violence does not rest with pupils and students. Some Black teachers have also experienced it. It is bad enough when it comes from colleagues, but is totally frustrating and humiliating when it comes from the children whom they are supposed to be teaching and where the discipline in the school is so weak that remedies seem impossible. Increasingly in areas of high racial harassment and violence, Black teachers find that even in schools where there are above average numbers of Black children, racial harassment and violence can still be a fairly common feature of everyday occurrences.

THE COLLAPSE OF THE YOUTH SERVICE

One consequence of the continued financial pressure on local government has been the almost total collapse of what used to be known as the Youth and Community Service. Local authority run youth clubs have virtually disappeared. There has also been less money available to assist voluntary sponsored youth initiatives. Local authorities have therefore been forced out of a very crucial part of adolescent development and a vital rung in the ladder of community coherence has been removed.

While this is a global problem, it is particularly devastating in some areas of the Black community where the opportunity to develop self-confidence, team spirit, leadership skills and a range of other skills so necessary in later life are crucial to the overall enhancement of the community's fortunes. A society that fails to invest in its youth signals its own death knell. The Youth Service which was generally seen as a sort of Cinderella service had little chance of surviving the savage cuts of the 1980s.

Yet, no one has undertaken a serious study of the damage done to society by their collapse. It is one thing to decide on the closure of the youth centre, but what do you do about the young people? They certainly do not go away. How many of them has society lost to any form of useful existence? While not seeking to establish a causal link, it cannot but be noticed that the increase in criminal activity among the 18-24 years old has tended to mirror the decline in effective local authority youth services. What a price!

HIGHER EDUCATION
We shall shortly be getting the first set of comprehensive official statistics on racial distribution in higher education. These would cast some real light both on the access to courses, the spread of courses being taken and the types of degrees being obtained. Since the polytechnics have now all become universities, these statistics will also allow us to see whether or not the switch to universities by the polytechnics has had any real adverse effect on the chances of Black people.

It will take a little longer to assess whether employer prejudice in favour of the University as opposed to the Polytechnic has been in anyway reduced by the switch. A study of 33 Polytechnics and Colleges published in 1987 confirmed the hitherto anecdotal evidence of under representation of ethnic minority groups in higher education. It also demonstrated that even when ethnic minority individuals gained access to higher education, the acquisition of a degree did not necessarily lead to a good job as employers might be operating discriminatory systems and criteria which mitigated against them.[6]

Asian students in higher education are about six times greater than either the number of African or African-Caribbean students. The most popular course for Asian students being Electrical and Electronic Engineering, Science and Pharmacy, the least popular being Humanities. For African-Caribbean students the most popular courses seem to be Economics, Law, Social Studies, Science and Applied Chemistry while the least popular are Humanities, Librarianship and Environmental Studies.

Discrimination in finding a job adequate to their qualification was one cause for continuing their studies after graduation. As a result ethnic minority graduates are more likely to continue their studies than their White counterparts. When they do this they are more likely than White students to take a higher degree. White students who stay on are likely to be taking a professional qualification.

By and large Asian and African-Caribbean students perceived their courses as being of greater personal benefit both in terms of self-development as well as achieving their goals than do a comparable group of White students.

Asian students are more likely than White students to move straight from secondary education to higher education. African-Caribbean students are less likely than either Asian or White students to go direct from secondary school to higher education. About 40% of African-Caribbean, 35 per cent of White and less than 20 per cent of Asian students had worked before beginning their higher education where that education was undertaken at a Polytechnic or College of Higher Education. Fewer people engaged in paid employment before entering

47

the older universities and it will be a matter of interest to see how the switch by Polytechnics to Universities has affected that process.

One other change has been that once they became Universities most of the Polytechnics dropped their access courses which had provided a second chance for so many people, especially those from ethnic minority groups, who had missed out first time round.

SELF-HELP AND COMMUNITY CHOICE

The government has made a virtue out of choice. It claims it is putting parents into the driving seat of the education train. The Muslim and Hindu groups have taken them at their word and have sought grant-aided status for their schools.

Yusuf Islam, Chairman of the Association of Muslim Schools, has expressed his disappointment at the government's continued refusal to grant voluntary aided status to any of their schools. He said "The government promotes Choice and Diversity in education and yet consistently refuses to offer Muslim parents the same educational choice afforded to Christians and Jews." Britain boasts that it is in the vanguard of multiracialism in Europe, yet Ireland, Denmark and Holland have all already grant aided Muslim schools.

The continual refusal by Britain to grant aid Muslim schools is therefore all the more reprehensible and defies all logic and sense of fair play. Muslims are the largest non-Christian minority in the country and have demonstrated their commitment to education through establishing almost 50 schools and colleges from their own resources. What they seek is not a favour but the exercise of justice. Theirs is a fair claim and should be met in fairness. The government may be assured that Muslim schools will not go away and it cannot forever shirk its duty by denying them their rights.

Not only is the government bound by its own legislation and rhetoric, it is also bound by the terms of the international documents to which it is a signatory. These documents ensure the right of parents to choose the kind of education their children receive.[7]

The UN Universal Declaration of Human Rights of 1948 states:

"Parents have a prior right to choose the kind of education that shall be given to their children."[8]

The European Parliament's Resolution on Freedom in Education in the European Community in 1984 states:

"Parents shall have the right to decide on the type of education and teaching to be given to their children...(and) the right to establish a school and provide instruction...it is in the duty of the state to provide

48

the necessary facilities for state or private schools."[9]

And finally, the European Parliament's Declaration of Fundamental Rights and Freedoms, 1989 states:

"Parents shall have the right to make provision for (such) education in accordance with their religious and philosophical convictions."[10]

So while the Muslim, Hindu, and the largely African-Caribbean London based Seventh-day Adventist schools wait, a number of Christian and Jewish schools have had their applications approved. Not a single Black ethnic minority application has ever been approved. Is government so amoral that no one can see the injustice? Can we not hope that in 1997, the European Year Against Racism, we will witness a beginning to the end of this wrong?

The network of supplementary schools run by African-Caribbean groups to assist children keep pace with their school work continues to grow and improve in quality. They have been invaluable benefits to hundred of children over the years. It is however important that African-Caribbean groups position themselves to take a greater involvement in the field of education and seek to establish and run schools in their own right. The Association of Supplementary School and the Caribbean Teachers Association should combine to develop a Caribbean Educational Trust with the function of setting up and running a number of schools and thus ensuring that African-Caribbean children have a genuine option in respect of their education.

In addition to the Saturday schools, African-Caribbean groups have conducted a number of evening classes, summer schools and individual tuition schemes, but much of their efforts had been supported by local authority grants, and owing to the financial position of most of the grant-giving authorities, they are now severely curtailed. More than two-thirds of the groups which were operating in the early eighties no longer exist.

In the shift to contract negotiations most self help groups working in the field of education faced new problems. They were trying to help some of the most disadvantaged youngsters to rebuild their self confidence and self image, and this created difficulties in getting appropriate performance indicators agreed. Purchasers seldom seemed to appreciate what it took to work with groups where a high percentage were low achievers needing substantial support and often demanded unrealistic outputs.

SOME FORMAL INVESTIGATIONS
The Commission for Racial Equality has conducted a number of formal

investigations into various practices in education. One is reported here because of the very special issues which it raised.

The 1980 Education Act made provision for parental choice of school. In 1988 a White parent in Cleveland made a request to have a child transferred to a different school with more White pupils. The child was attending a school, which the parent admitted was a good school but had 40 per cent of Asian and 60 per cent of White pupils. The parent's request was to have the child removed to a school with 98 per cent White pupils.

The education authority recognised that the request was based on racial grounds but was advised that legally it had to decide in favour of the request under the rights of choice, granted under the 1980 Education Act, even though they concluded that it was contrary to its own equal opportunity policy.

After an Investigation in 1989, The Commission for Racial Equality took the view that the Race Relations Act 1976 overrode the Education Act 1980 and that in granting the request the education authority had breached the Race Relations Act. The CRE stated that:

(a) LEA's in carrying out their functions under the 1980 Education Act, must not discriminate
(b) Complying with a parent's request for a transfer based on racial grounds constitutes racial segregation, which is unlawful under the Race Relations Act 1976.[11]

The Commission served notice of its findings of unlawful discrimination to the Secretary of State for Education asking him to ensure that Cleveland and other Local Education Authorities did not comply with parental preferences made on racial grounds. The Secretary of State rejected the Commission's findings and the Commission sought a judicial review of the Secretary of States' decision.

Senior citizens go about their daily routine in the pleasant atmosphere of the Clive Lloyd House

Politically aware members of racial and cultural
minorities are now increasingly asserting their rights
to appropriate services. They maintain that they are
ratepayers and taxpayers too!"

Shama Ahmed

CHAPTER FOUR

THE HEALTH, SOCIAL SERVICES AND WELFARE CRISIS

THE NATIONAL HEALTH SERVICE

Many Black people arrived in Britain to work in the National Health Service. They were involved in all areas of the Service as doctors, nurses, technicians and basic support staff. Yet at every level they have encountered discrimination. Because of the numbers involved and the fact that some Black staff have made some progress it is not always apparent that an unacceptable level of discrimination is at play throughout the service.

There are scores of Industrial Tribunal cases to illustrate the depth of the problems. The Commission for Racial Equality established that selection processes for entrance to medical training were flawed and operated against equal access to medical training by many aspiring Black applicants. The largest proportion of ethnic minority doctors in the Service came from the Asian sub-continent and despite nearly fifty years of dedicated service during which time they should have gained acknowledgement of their place in the Service, many are still experiencing difficulty in promotion. Those who do invariably excel in their specialities.

The position of nurses is no better. Okyne-Turkson, a Ghanian won his industrial tribunal case against the Macclesfield Health Authority in 1989 for failure to gain promotion to charge nurse. None of the sixteen nurses shortlisted for interview for six vacancies was Black. The tribunal accepted that Turkson who was not even shortlisted was the most experienced and qualified of the applicants. He had nine years experience as a staff nurse and had on a number of occasions performed satisfactorily as an acting charge nurse. Four of the six White nurses appointed had less than two years experience as staff nurses. His employers claimed he had not demonstrated leadership qualities during his functioning as a staff nurse.

The Health Service is being reorganised into a series of independent Trusts, and like every other reorganisation and restructuring exercise that has occurred over the past 17 years of the current Conservative period of government the issues of equal opportunity have been ignored. Black staff have suffered to a greater extent as a result of these exercises.

But it is not only staff who have suffered. One of the other changes was the introduction of budget holding GPs who were able to purchase treatment for their patients directly from providers. Fewer doctors serving areas predominantly occupied by Black communities are budget holders and few Black GPs are themselves budget holders. This places the majority of Black patients in the slow lane of a two track health service. This is of particular relevance to the Black elderly, a large number of whom had contributed so much to the development of the National Health Service and hoped like the rest of society that when the time came, the Service in all its fullness would be there for them on an equal basis.

BLACK ELDERLY
Britain's Black elderly currently comprise just under 6% of the Black population. This compares with 20.9% of the White population being elderly. This reflects the varying immigration patterns which has given rise to the elderly in different ethnic communities developing at different rates. Asian groups brought in larger numbers of elderly dependants to provide earlier family support and stability. African and Caribbean elderly emerged through growing old in this country. With the cessation of primary immigration, this has now peaked and a more stable rate of growth is emerging.

TABLE 7. Black elderly growth in the UK with projection to 2010.

	1981	1995	Projected 2010
African/Caribbean	15000	65500	165000
Indian	34000	61000	195000
Pakistani/Bangladeshi	17000	31000	105000
Other ethnic groups	10000	28500	90000
All minority ethnic groups	76000	186000	555000

Those responsible for developing care packages for the elderly need to take these trends into consideration, but in many cases they have not. With local authority budgets severely compressed, and with community care so dependent on need assessments, any inability to respond sensitivity to culturally driven priorities may adversely affect assessment outcomes. Where a community is short on advocacy skills and where community structures are weak and unable to cope with the contract culture that has replaced the grant culture, their elderly are likely to suffer as larger White organisations see the small Black groups as pawns in their quest for scarce resources but not as genuine allies in the delivery of services. Hence they will contract with local authorities to deliver services to the Black communities. Some have incorporated Black people into the planning, delivery and evaluation process but many have been proceeding on the paternalistic "we know best" principle.

A number of Black self help projects have been developed to provide luncheon clubs and day centres which are community based. Black led housing associations have created, generally in conjunction with larger White associations, a number of sheltered housing units but they have been unable to keep pace with the rise of numbers among the Black elderly.

With the collapse of many of the jobs with which the Black communities had been traditionally associated, an increasing number have approached retirement age having already been out of work for five years or more. Having worked hard from their early twenties for 30-35 years, they have suddenly found themselves made redundant in their mid to late fifties and compulsory retirement forced upon them prematurely. Increasingly, those from the Caribbean area who can afford it are selling up and returning home. But many are not in that situation and must stay. The community will have to rediscover its support mechanisms if the Black elderly are not to find their final years, a period of despair and isolation.

MENTAL HEALTH

Susannah Strong commenting on the Audit Commission's report on mental health services for adults had this to say:

> *"If as much time, energy and commitment was put into ensuring a decent mental health service as is devoted to producing reports about the lack of one, we would have a cracker. Every report was pinpointed similar trouble spots."[1]*

In fact, the issues are not new. It is not the case for Community Care that is flawed, but the inability to make the resources both financial and human available to make the system work which has created the problems. Liz Sayce, policy director of MIND and a member of the Audit Commission's advisory panel argues that money is still being spent on expensive hospital care when it could be more effectively spent in the community. This is open to considerable debate, but she is nearer the mark when she contends that "there must be a serious willingness to develop joint services that users and relatives want."

It is obvious that if Community Care is bedevilled in its attempts to meet the needs of the mentally ill in general,[2] then the plight of the Black mentally ill will be that much worse. It was so before community care came in, and it remains so. There are several facts which almost every practitioner knows. Black people are over-represented in psychiatric wards when compared with their White counterparts. They are more likely to be over-medicated and diagnosed as suffering from schizophrenia or another form of psychotic illness. They are also more likely to be removed by police to a place of safety under section 136 of the Mental Health Act 1983, and detained in locked wards of psychiatric hospitals. They are less likely to get appropriate diagnosis or treatment at an early stage of their illness. They are also less likely to get psychotherapy or counselling. In short, they operate at a point below the national standards of care.

While practitioners acknowledge the low level of take up of mental health support services by Black people, they seem not to have been able to develop effective strategies for providing and delivering services to Black people with mental health problems. Section 11 of the Mental Health Act 1983 provides for families to be involved in the care provision for their relatives who have been diagnosed as mentally ill. This assumes a partnership between the professionals and the family based on trust and mutual respect working across cultural and linguistic boundaries. Many have found this a bridge too far and feeling unprepared to meet the challenge it posed have left the family and mentally ill person to their own devices.

Those who have taken up the challenge have been able to get some exciting results, but have often felt isolated and unsupported. Section 117 of the Mental Health Act promotes a multi-disciplinary approach to after-care provision. This means agencies working together and jointly providing the necessary resources. This is more difficult in the current management culture of purchaser/provider splits with each agency looking to hold on to as much of the resources as it can.

It took the death of a musician Jonathan Zito at the hands of Christopher Clunis and a very highly publicised campaign to get the usual response. If faced with an uncomfortable situation, set up an enquiry and hope that by the time the report is published the problem has evaporated. The Ritchie report, the enquiry into the care and treatment of Christopher Clunis, could well fall into that category.

What was interesting about the report came in a small section captioned "ethnic minorities". In it the report states "we have not come across any prejudice or discrimination in relation to Christopher Clunis." But may one ask, were they looking for it? Are they really

56

asking the public to believe that the care and treatment Christopher Clunis received was in every material regard the same as a White mentally ill person would have received? Was this the unanimous view of the entire enquiry team? There are obviously unanswered questions and the statement raises more doubts than it clarifies.

The Richie report inspired another report. This came from the Race Equality Unit of the National Institute of Social Work. It was called "A review of the Clunis Inquiry: A Black Perspective." This latter review clearly felt there was enough evidence to support a conclusion of discrimination. In common with so many other Black people, Clunis had been subjected to high dosage of drugs even against his protest. He had requested but not been given either psychotherapy or counselling. There was no engagement with his family as Section 117 of the Mental Health Act would have required and he was treated outside of his catchment area.

But Christopher Clunis is not alone. He singly got more publicity than the others. Between 1992 and 1995 over a score of other Black men have as a consequence of inadequate care and support committed violent offences and have been given custodial sentences. The sadness is that, with proper support, they could most likely have been still in the community.

The London Borough of Lambeth has produced a practice guide for its staff working with Black people with mental health difficulties. They have also linked up with the "Black and Asian Mental Health Forum" in order to provide greater community involvement in developing their mental health strategy. A project with a similar set of objectives was established in Lewisham in 1994. It was jointly funded for two years in the first instance by the Kings Fund, Lewisham Social Services Department and Lewisham and Guy's Mental Health Trust.

Gyan Dass the first project coordinator of the Roshni Ghar project in Keighley in outlining the need for the project said she wanted to challenge some of the myths which were in circulation about the Asian community and mental health. One of the most persistent was the idea that there were no mental health problems in the Asian community. Another was that the extended family took care of everything. Yet another was that Asian men would not accept a mental health project for their wives, sisters or daughters. None of these was true, she insisted. While the project received financial help from Bradford Social Services, more came from the Health Service. Not even when the community tries to develop culturally sensitive services does it get the recognition and support it deserves.

Addressing the Royal College of Psychiatrists on 21 February 1996 on a report by the World Health Organisation, Professor Julian Leff told his audience that stigma and a lack of strong family networks meant

57

that only 15% of schizophrenics in the West were likely to make a good recovery from the first attack of their illness compared with 37% of those in underdeveloped countries.3 He added that while 14% of Schizophrenics in Dublin and 29% in Nottingham could expect to have good outcomes after two years; 51% of those in Ibadan, Nigeria and 54% in Agra, North India would recover. The low points were Honolulu (3.5%) Nagasaki (5.7%) and Moscow (7.9%). He continued:

"In the West, about one in four people recover very well from a first attack of the illness and remain well for many years. In non-Western countries the outcome is conspicuously better; about one in two people do well."

Societies with a strong sense of duty and a network of people to share the burden of support as well as the emotional and physical care demands greatly assist the sufferer's recovery. Similarly, cultures which are less confrontational, more cooperative and less competitive, with greater opportunities for involvement and participation allowing "sufferers to feel they are contributing to the economy" and to feel valued, add to the likelihood of recovery. These observations together with a possible genetic link made a very dim prospect for Black sufferers in Britain unless their communities give the issue a higher priority than they have so far given.

CHILD CARE ISSUES

Any discussion of child care issues is incomplete without some analysis of the balance of families with dependant children. Some 65% of Pakistani/Bangladeshi families have dependant children, but only 5% are lone parent families. When we compared this with African/Caribbean families we found 43% having dependant children but a staggering 20% being lone parent families. The details for other groups are set out in the table below.

TABLE 8. Families with dependant children by ethnic group, Winter 1994/95

	Couples	Lone	Families with dependant children
Pakistani/Bangladeshi	60	5	65
India	49	2	51
White	24	4	28
Black	23	20	43
Other	39	6	45
All ethnic groups	27	4	31

Source: Labour Force Survey. Central Statistical Office

58

One parent families constitute almost half (46.5%) of all African/Caribbean families with dependant children. Only 4% of Indian families with dependant children are one parent families. For White families the figure is 14% and for Pakistani/Bangladeshi families it is 7.5%. While no direct causal link has been established, there is a correlation between these figures and the incidence of children in care. There are other contributing factors to the breakdown of family cohesion leading to children being accommodated. When this becomes necessary the chances of rehabilitation of the child and reunion of families will depend on recognition of cultural and religious background and expectations.

One of the successes of the Commission for Racial Equality was to convince government of the need to take into account the ethnic origins of children in need in local areas when developing service plans. The Children Act 1989 now requires that in making fostering placements and adoption decisions the authority must take into account the linguistic background of the child as well as issues of race, culture and religion.

The level of Black children accommodated remains disproportionately high but as yet no serious national research has been undertaken to determine the underlying causes. The plight of Black children hits the agenda mostly in cases where the media gets involved when a high profile case emerges which focuses on the dilemmas posed by the advocates of same-race placements and those of trans-racial placements.

There is a wealth of anecdotal evidence to support the claim that many services are failing to provide care programmes that offer Black children accommodated a positive self image of themselves. There is something wrong if Black young people leave care ashamed of their blackness and yet this so often happens. Nationally Black children are two and a half times more likely to enter the care system than White children.

There are a few Black-in-Care Centres springing up over the country. Their principal benefit would be to create models of care excellence which might be documented and used more widely as training for care workers. The problems of Black young people in care will not be resolved fully until all social workers are able to work effectively across the board with Black young people. What the Black-in-Care Unit is able to do is destroy the myths that have developed surrounding working with Black young people and demonstrate the potential for change that exists.

The issue has been shrouded with such a level of negativism that administrators and planners alike approach it in a mood of defeat and hopelessness. All young people leaving care regardless of the colour of their skin do have problems; but Black young people have all the additional problems posed by racial prejudice and discrimination. These are not always recognised and acknowledged. Wandsworth Social Services Department runs a highly rated care leaver scheme to prepare young people for the time when they leave care. It is known as the Wandsworth Independent Living Scheme.

But nothing has illustrated the confusion surrounding Black children in need of care more succinctly than the issues of fostering and adoption. Every adoption agency can point to disasters. Bringing up young people is not a perfect science. Many natural parents have disasters too. So no one should be surprised that some placements fail given the lack of genuine support foster parents get in this very difficult and sensitive area.

The Children Act 1989 having given the green light for ethnic and religious considerations to be drawn into fostering and adoption decisions, the debate over same-race and different-race placements took off to new intensity. The Health department circular says:

"Other things being equal, placement with a family of similar ethnic origin and religion is most likely to meet a child's need as fully as possible."

Later in 1993 following a number of high profile cases, it sought to clarify its advice by saying that "race should not necessarily be more influential than any other factor." The dogmatists missed out two essential phases in the advice. Firstly "other things being equal" and "most likely". Very often things were not equal in that they did not have a Black family ready and willing to undertake the adoption. They were often dealing with a situation in which some level of bonding had taken place. It seems singularly brutal, unfeeling and uncaring to say to a family that has been fostering a child for three or four years, that they are unfit, on grounds of race only, to adopt.

Secondly, "most likely" only states a probability not a certainty. It does not establish a same-race only policy, but merely seeks to lay down a preference, but only if other things are equal. The policy was therefore quite clear. It was only the attempt to highjack the policy that caused the disputes. Two of which are worth noting.

Dave and Margaret Tyler had fostered Cheryl since she was four months old. They had fostered more than 70 children over a 20 year period and two thirds of them were Black or Asian. Avon Social Services Department evidently considered them a valued resource or so they thought until they sought to adopt Cheryl after five years.

It took three years of political and legal fighting before they were allowed to adopt Cheryl. During this time, they had to complete a

Black cultural awareness project during which they were taught to use the phrase "coffee with milk" instead of "black coffee" and at one group session they had to join in singing "Baa Baa Green Sheep."

James and Roma Lawrence are a middle-class mixed race couple who were turned down as potential adopters because they did not have sufficient racial awareness. This followed an answer Roma Lawrence gave to the White social worker who interviewed her. She alleged that she had not experienced any racial discrimination in the county town where she lived. Angrily she described the policy that led to their rejection as one put together by militant Blacks and guilt-ridden Whites.

There are far more Black children in care than there are potential Black adopters so for a long time yet there will be a deficit in Black families. In these circumstances is it really in the interest of those young lives that they should be committed to residential care? No doubt While families bringing up Black children need to appreciate the impact discrimination is likely to have on their lives and to be sensitive enough to seek to learn how best to guide their charges through those treacherous waters. But they are not going to learn those very important lessons by entering the realms of the ridiculous where "black coffee" becomes "coffee without milk". The objective ought to be finding ways of helping White adopters make the best of an already difficult job not making it harder for them to succeed. At the same time by all means increase the number of potential Black adopters, but let the children come first.

RACE AND SOCIAL WORK TRAINING

Over the past decade race has become an increasing focus in Social Work training. The Central Council for Education and Training in Social Work (CCETSW) had accepted the need for the involvement of a number of Black professionals and created a Black Perspective Group. They became the driving force behind what CCETSW did in the area of race. They failed however to recognise the link between CCETSW and the government. It was not a free agent.

When they persuaded CCETSW to include in Annex 5 Paper 30 (the document setting out the requirements to the Diploma in Social Work) a statement that "racism is endemic in the values, attitudes and structures of British society" they pushed the boat out too far for CCETSW's sponsors. This offended the government, the *Daily Mail* had a field day, and not everybody at CCETSW was prepared to defend it. Some were quite prepared to admit that had it not been for the Black Perspectives Group it would not have been said. Annex 5 continued:

"CCETSW recognises the effects of racism on Black people are incompatible with the values of social work and therefore seeks to combat racist practices in all areas of its responsibilities. In order to achieve the DipSW students must demonstrate that they identify and deal with discrimination, racism, disadvantage, inequality and injustice."

Brave words but who would see that all this was done. Were the Colleges and Universities ready to take on this role? Could CCETSW monitor it? The Government had its answer. A new chairman for CCETSW was due and they sent in Jeffrey Greenwood. He came with what was a clear brief to do away with what the government would describe as "political correctness."

The typical review was set in place and a restructuring exercise undertaken. Out went the Black Perspective Group. England, Scotland, Wales and Northern Ireland would each have their own national committee with responsibility for their own structures and sub-committees. It would be difficult for Black professionals to organise to respond to four national committees in any coherent fashion.

Facing criticism of the apparent downgrading of race issues, Tony Hall had this to say:

"As far as CCETSW is concerned, it has not gone soft on race. But attitudes change about the language which should be used to describe the problem. References to anti-racism and anti-discrimination were viewed by ministers as being too negative. We should aim to use language that clearly expresses what we mean. CCETSW is as committed as it always has been to issues of equal opportunity and discrimination."

His assurances are as good as CCETSW's history and past performance on equality.

Mono Chakrabarti expressing his concerns over the outcome of Black perspectives in the new arrangements says:

"I am also concerned to see how Black professionals are going to be recruited, nurtured and promoted within the Central Council as an organisation"[4]

HOUSING
Housing remains a central issue for Black families. However the overall position has improved over the last two decades. The struggle will be to

ensure how the residual problems are handled in a climate of deregulation and to focus on those groups in greatest need. A look at the size of family households will give a broad picture of the relative housing needs of the various ethnic groups.

TABLE 9. Ethnic group of head of household by household size, Spring 1995

	One Persons	Two People	Three People	Four People	Five People	Six or more People	All (Thousands)
White	28	34	16	15	5	2	22.548
Black[2]	31	29	20	12	4	4	375
Indian	9	17	20	26	16	12	265
Pakistani/Bangladeshi	8	11	14	21	15	31	163
Other[3]	28	22	20	19	6	5	239
All ethnic groups	29	34	16	15	5	2	23597

2. Includes Caribbean, African and other Black people of non-mixed origin.
3. Includes Chinese, other ethnic groups and non-mixed groups and people of mixed origin.

Source: Labour Force Survey. CSO

While at the lower end of demand on large housing only 7% of White households have five or more people, some 46% or nearly half of all Pakistani/Bangladeshi households have five or more people. We have seen elsewhere that they are the ones facing the highest pressure in the job market and have the highest percentage of economically inactive and this would be bound to add pressure on the access to suitable housing for their families. Both the Indian and Pakistani/Bangladeshi groups have fewer single person households and this may reflect greater family cohesion.

Indian households have a higher house ownership than any other group. Among the Indian Community home ownership is 84%. This compares with 67% for White households 61% for Pakistani and Bangladeshi and 40% for Black (African and Caribbean) households who lead the social sector housing with 52%. Whereas 1 in 2 Black households use social sector housing, 1 in 4 White households do so. While among the Asian groups 1 in 4 Pakistani/Bangladeshi households use social sector housing for Indian households the ratio is 1 in 14. Full details of housing tenure is set out below.

TABLE 10. Ethnic group of head of household by tenure 1993/94

	OWNED		RENTED	
	Outright	with Mortgages	from social sector	Privately
Ethnic Minority Group				
Indian	20	64	7	9
Pakistian/Bangladeshi	13	48	24	15
Black	6	34	52	8
Others	12	36	33	20
All ethnic minority groups	12	45	31	12
White	26	41	24	9
All ethnic groups	25	1	25	9

Source: General Household Survey. Office of Population Census and Surveys.

It is also worth noting that the Indian group is the only one which as a percentage of its own group is more involved in the privately rented sector than social sector housing. Another set of useful figures are those relating to overcrowding.

TABLE 11. Overcrowding: by ethnic group of head of household 1993/94

	Spare Bedroom	Equal Bedroom Standard	Overcrowding
White	68	29	3
West Indian	45	45	10
Indian	56	33	11
Pakistani/Bangladeshi	34	35	31

Source: Office of Population Census and Surveys.

Almost a third of Pakistani/Bangladeshi households live in overcrowded conditions. Compared with just 3% of White households. At the other end of the spectrum two-thirds of White households have above standard bedroom accommodation compared with one-third for Pakistani/Bangladeshi households. If we compare these figures with the levels of home ownership it is evident that not all owner occupiers are in adequate housing.

64

Although less blatant than it was two decades ago Black people still have difficulty in getting mortgages from Banks and Building Societies on the same terms as White people. This is a very complex issue, and much is based on lender perception of the borrower's status and credit worthiness, the location of the property and its potential for holding its value. It is a maze in which there are very favourable conditions for the exercise of prejudice.

There is nothing new about homelessness, but it has grown into a very serious problem for some young Black people. Nearly half of those seeking advice from agencies dealing with homelessness in London are Black and two-thirds of these are under 25 years of age. The Black community is faced with a mounting body of homeless young people who having left home spend a period sleeping on a friend's floor, move on from one bed and breakfast establishment to another, never staying in one place long enough to resolve their housing problem. In London Black young people are four times more likely to be homeless than their White counterparts.[5]

The changes in Social Security regulations are adding even greater pressure on young Black homeless people. The restrictions placed on local government as part of Central government strategy to drive local government out of the housing market will adversely affect not only those who had traditionally used social sector housing as their main housing source, but will remove all hope from those who find themselves homeless.

Organisations like CHAR (Campaign for the Homeless and Rootless) Shelter and SHAC (Sheltered Housing Aid Centre) while fighting homelessness in a general sense are not sufficiently seized of the special factors contributing to Black homelessness nor of the consequences to the community of its continued growth. Local authorities when they exercised total control over the social sector of housing responded to these needs by supporting community initiatives and by the mid-seventies had established a network of responses which were beginning to come to grips with the problem. CHAR, Shelter and SHAC are national organisations and do not have the same level of accountability as a local authority has and as a consequence are less responsive.

As the stress of homelessness builds up over the months the victims are likely to suffer both physical and mental deterioration in their health. This increases the social costs and adds to the demands that are likely to be made on already overstretched services.

Housing Associations are talking over more of the local authorities 'social sector' function in housing. Some of them have begun to accept that they must also take on the responsibility of providing social housing for the most disadvantaged groups within the Black communities. The Housing Corporation has failed in its support for Black initiatives and has undermined years of hard work by concerned Black people in Birmingham in the way it handled the Harambee Housing Association. Few public bodies have operated with such disregard for the needs of Black people.

Racial harassment in housing remains a general problem but in certain areas where the activities of the British National Party and similar Right-wing organisations are in evidence, the harassment is considerably heightened. Most local authorities have developed policies for dealing with racial harassment and a number have been successful in gaining eviction orders or other restraining orders against those tenants who were guilty of harassment.

The CRE has been able through formal investigations, research activity and support to complainants to identify continuing racial discrimination at all levels and in all sections of the housing market. Statutory codes of practice now exist for both the rented and non-rented sectors of housing.

SOCIAL SECURITY

As people live longer the pensions element of the Social Security bill increases. The more people we keep unemployed, the greater the cost. As the whole spectrum of costs which are met by the Social Security budget increased the government became aware that unless some curb could be found, the point would come when existing funds would not be able to meet demand. At the Conservative Conference in 1994, the party announced an assault on fraud, but it also launched an attack on those vulnerable groups - single parents - unemployed young people and asylum seekers.

What is significant is that not only are these groups the most vulnerable in society but that a disproportionate number of them are Black. The government has continued its ad hoc approach to Social Security rather than taking a comprehensive review. It has not examined the impact of its regulations on Black claimants. Although the agency is supposed to be following Citizen Charter principles it is not fully equipped with interpreting and translating facilities to meet the demand of its multi-lingual customers.

Black claimants were further disadvantaged by the closure of many of the smaller local offices which tended to specialise in dealing with claimants' enquiries. The Freeline, the agency freephone service which dealt with 2.5 million claimant inquiries per annum was scrapped and out-of-hours emergency services abolished. People were expected to programme their emergencies to fit into office hours. Perhaps we should have renamed the agency Social Insecurity.

"There will be no Black commanders,
or Black superintendents of police if there
were no Black constables."

Lord Pitt of Hampstead
4 February 1982

CHAPTER FIVE

LAW AND ORDER

THE CRIMINAL JUSTICE SYSTEM

With the Conservative Party in power since 1979 we have never been far removed from the Law and Order debate. True though it is that party leaders and their propagandists have sought to raise the issue in the most emotive terms whenever the party has faced electoral declines or slumped in the opinion polls. So sensitive is the issue, that New Labour has made a conscious bid to take the high ground by proclaiming through its leader Tony Blair, that it would be "tough on crime and tough on the causes of crime".

But how do Black people fair in the Criminal Justice System? There are several parts to the system and each is developing its own response to the demands of racial justice. This has tended to provide difficulty in identifying where the problems are most heavily located and how best to set about solutions.

What we expect from a criminal justice system is fairness. Equality before the law must not be merely a slogan, it must be a reality. In other words, there must be an equality of experience. But despite over thirty years of race relations legislation, the response of the several parts of the justice system has been so sporadic and uneven, that we are far from any semblance of a genuinely multi-racial criminal justice system.

Much of the debate so far has been dominated by the position of Black people as the recipient of the Criminal Justice System. Their treatment has been analysed again and again, and always with the same results. One is reminded of the conclusion arrived at by Nagal and Neef in the light of 50 years of research in the United States of America:

"Whatever the truth is about racial discrimination in the judicial process, the truth will be found more by a sceptical, questioning

analysis than by an eagerness to accept that which appears to be true, or that which we would like to think is true."[1]

This implies the need for an open debate in the quest for a consensus on the many issues that do arise. This would be greatly enhanced by more Black people participating in the various levels of the administration of the justice system - police, lawyers, magistrates, judges, court officials, prison officers and probation officers. A genuine multi-racial interaction at all levels could then be envisaged resulting in the general enrichment of the system.

The absence of Black people at the several levels of the system has kept alive suspicions of its integrity and raised questions both in respect of equality of process and equity of outcomes. Waters (1988) argues that "all personnel in a multi-racial criminal justice system would be racially aware, generating a sympathetic climate and possessing a repertoire of skills and knowledge in dealing with defendants from a wide variety of cultures" . He adds quite rightly:

"Racial awareness cannot be forced upon people, but it can be nurtured and the right sort of conditions can be generated for its development. It seems unlikely, in a British context, that such a system would ever be based on formal segregation, but would rather be permeated by notions of cultural pluralism."[2]

Section 95 of the Criminal Justice Act 1991 places a duty on the Secretary of State to publish information annually for the purpose of "facilitating the performance of such persons of their duty to avoid discrimination against persons on the grounds of race or sex or any other improper ground." The law thus starts to give legitimacy to some form of differentiation on grounds of race, and culture. This is a challenging concept for a system that has prided itself on its resistance to change.

Another requirement of the Act is that Courts are bound when sentencing young persons to consider their maturity. This is a vital factor in choosing the appropriate penalty. This is of particular importance as there is a necessity to understand the ways in which culture may affect societal values and hence what are perceived as the norms of maturity.

Every part of the system is responding with the collection of data and the creation of anti-racist policies of one form or another. While it is generally accepted that racial disadvantage and discrimination are widespread, personal and institutional acceptance is less acknowledged. Most people see others as being responsible and the Criminal Justice System, as a system, has been among the last to come to terms with the situation. After all it is there to dispense "justice" and discrimination and prejudice are the very antithesis to what it is about.

That is not to say that parts of the system have not responded earlier than others; but to restate the fact that a system is as strong as its weakest part. It is therefore important that all parts of the system are geared up to deal with the consequences of the increase in social disadvantage experienced by Black people as a result of the Thatcher years as well as the increase in racial abuse and harassment of Black people throughout Europe as the growth of neo-facism sweeps across the continent.

It is not being argued that a culturally sensitive multi-racial criminal justice system could reverse the increase in racial disadvantage and discrimination. What is none-the-less true is that the absence of such a system will ensure a considerable worsening of the situation. The stakes are high. The research of the Policy Studies Institute (1983) has examined the mutual mistrust between young Black people and the system and documented the areas of friction.

What has emerged is the linkage of particular ethnic groups with particular types of crime and the consequent targeting and policing of those communities in a particular way. This has resulted in the predictable response from sentencers producing the inevitable racially differential outcomes represented in the growing numbers in prison and or probation. Britain is fast approaching United States proportions for the Black people passing through the Criminal Justice System. We are entering a vicious negative spiral that will require more than good intentions to halt.

THE POLICE
Serving police officers at the level of Chief Constables and Deputies have always affirmed their commitment to equality of treatment for Black citizens. They have generally supported a range of initiatives to recruit Black officers into their forces and then to improve dialogue between themselves and the Black communities in their areas. Indeed, by any objective assessment, the police forces will be seen to have put more effort and spent more money on equal opportunity objectives than most other public service agencies.

In addition to local force training, there is the Home Office sponsored national training in race equality. It was first centred on Brunel University but later deemed to be too theoretical and subsequently contracted to Equality Associates as being able to provide a more community centred and practical experience. The Home Office provided in excess of £500,000 per year to this training. John Major during the 1992 election campaign praised the project particularly mentioning the weekend placement scheme whereby police officers on

71

the course went to spend a weekend with a Black family. There are those who have been waiting to see the occasion when it would be organised for a Black person to spend a weekend with a White police officer and his/her family.

In a democracy where the accepted standard is governance by consent it is essential that the community and police must share a body of trust if satisfactory policing is to be achieved. Senior police officers have acknowledged that one ingredient in that process is to improve the balance of Black police officers. But many in the Black community remain unconvinced about the welcome they are likely to receive from peer groups in the force coupled with a fear of what they might be asked to condone by way of treatment to their own community.

Lord Pitt of Hampstead in addressing the House of Lords during the debate on the Scarman Report in February 1982 urged the Black community to realise how important the police were to them, and how important it was to have Black people in positions of authority at every level of society. He added that there would be no Black commanders or Black superintendents if there were no Black constables. Many heeded his advise to join, sadly the drop out rate has been uncomfortably high.

There are two other issues that seriously undermine the efforts of chief officers. One is the treatment many Black people encounter in their dealings with police. This can range from abuse and disrespect when stopped by an officer, through wrongful arrest to death in the police cell. No amount of apologies, seldom received, or financial settlement can remove the trauma of some of these experiences. The second is the fact that many feel that in cases where Black people are the victims police are less successful in making arrests and gaining convictions than where Black people are the perpetrators of the crime.

On the 24 February 1982, the Observer carried a story of a Nigerian student who was asleep in the back of a Cortina driven by his friend when the car was stopped by a number of police officers. The student was dragged from the car, kicked in the testicles and stomach, bundled into a police van and put in a cell. Calling out in pain because of his injuries, he was eventually seen by a doctor who ordered his immediate removal to hospital. Before being removed he was charged with "being drunk in a public place". As a result of his injuries he had to have one testicle removed. The case against him was dismissed by the magistrate and he subsequently lodged a formal complaint against the two officers who had assaulted him.

The investigation of his complaint concluded that he had in fact been assaulted but it would be impossible to establish which officers were guilty. Both the DPP and the Police Complaints Board accepted that view and no disciplinary action was taken. With a clean record the officers were on their way to promotion.

So incensed by this was the Black community that the 50,000 strong Confederation of Indian Organisations issued the following statement:

"In the view of the widespread bias by the police force while investigating complaints against their colleagues, until the Home Office agrees to establish an independent board of inquiry to deal with such complaints, we are asking our members to actively discourage the ethnic minorities from joining the police force."[3]

On the 25 January 1996 an inquest jury returned a verdict of unlawful killing at the inquest into the death of Shiji Lapite a Nigerian seeking asylum. He died in custody at a police station. In this case he died from asphyxiation following a struggle with police who were arresting him on suspicion of possession of drugs. This is a claim vehemently denied by his family and friends who describe him as a deeply religious man who did not take drugs. The Coroner, Dr Stephen Chan, called upon Chief Police Officers to "ensure that all police officers are left in no doubt of the hazards and dangers of this practice". Lapite who had been held in a neck lock suffered a fracture to his voice box and some 45 separately identifiable injuries.

But he was not the first Black man to die in a police station following the application of head or neck locks. Winston Rose died in 1981, Nicholas Ofusu in 1983. Both of these were mentally ill. Then there was Oliver Pryce in 1995 in a Cleveland police station. There have been other mysterious deaths of Black people in police stations or during the process of arrest. Joy Garner died while being arrested by police on the direction of the immigration service who were seeking her deportation. Wayne Douglas alleged to have threatened police with a knife when he was arrested on suspicion of aggravated burglary died in police custody resulting in the 1995 Brixton riots. Post mortem examination determined death from a heart attack. What is not yet clear is what brought on the heart attack. The Police Complaints Authority are supervising the investigation into the circumstances surrounding Douglas's death.

These tragedies do not tell the whole story, although they have a severely negative accumulative effect on police Black relations. The police are an essential part of the fabric of our society and we all depend on them to ensure public safety. Ways must be found for the police to gain and maintain public support from all communities.

But as Sir Paul Condon, The Metropolitan Police Commissioner must now know, gaining community support can be loaded with hidden and not so hidden pitfalls. In the summer of 1995, he decided that the force would launch a concerted attack on muggings. Such research as his officers had done led them to the conclusion that most muggings in the London high crime areas were carried out by Black young men. Now this is entirely different from saying that most Black young men are muggers and in any dispassionate atmosphere the difference would be appreciated and understood.

However in his quest for community support he wrote a letter to a selected group of community "leaders" and representatives along with local and central government agencies to a meeting on July 28, 1995 at which he would seek to explain the strategy of the drive and enlist support. In his letter he ventured the view that most muggings in London were carried out by young Black men. Sir Paul who had arrived at the Metropolitan Police Service with a commitment to racial equality and up to then had been making some headway in gaining the confidence of the Black community suddenly found that once the letter had entered the public domain he was suddenly drawn into the eye of a storm.

Bernie Grant, the Black Labour MP for Tottenham, in an angry reaction said:

"People will just think that every Black person is a mugger because the Metropolitan Police Commissioner says so."[4]

But is this what he did say or even meant? Paul Boateng, the Black Labour MP for Brent South, raised the question:

"You can produce the same facts that show that the overwhelming majority of city fraud is committed by white middle-age upper class males. Are we going to have specific initiatives geared toward that section of the community?"[5]

The Commission for Racial Equality entered the fray. Its spokesperson said:

"We are concerned that the Commissioner's initiative may be a reaction to pressure from some police officers and others who have objected to the publicity surrounding concerns about the considerably over-representation of Black young men in stop and search figures."[6]

Mark Mettcalfe of the Hackney Colin Roach Centre said:

"His comments are just a cynical attempt to justify the alarming high rate of young Blacks already being stopped. To a Black person in Hackney getting stopped by police is part of daily life, like cleaning their teeth."[7]

74

Peter Herbert of the Society of Black Lawyers, again drew attention to the high number of Black people stopped and searched. He said:

"We have never been called to a meeting to discuss the problem of racially motivated attacks. I wonder if this is being done to cover up the fact that the majority of stop and searches by the police are on Black people."[8]

Pastor Frimpong Manson, Chairman of the Broadwater Farm Tenant's Association, in Tottenham said:

"Whatever he intended to say, he should have known how it would be interpreted. His media communications people should have been applying some wisdom here."[9]

Lord Scarman came to Sir Paul's defence. He said:

"I have tremendous sympathy with Sir Paul, because I don't think he has any racist intention to attack people just because they are Black. He has seen a problem, and has gone to the people who he thinks can help."[10]

There is always a problem in the use of statistics to advance an argument. Care must be taken to ensure that the correct set of statistics are selected and that those to whom the statistics are being directed have the reference points to allow intelligent and unambiguous interpretation. There is no doubt that Sir Paul felt confident about the accuracy of his statistics. What he did not do was to supply the recipients of his letter the reference points with which to interpret them.

For a start the statistics related to selected areas of London with a heavy Black population. They were not London wide figures. Secondly they were victim studies and needed to be assessed in that light, and thirdly they related to the number of muggings, not the number of muggers. Everybody knows that muggings whether perpetrated by Black or White are carried out by a small hard-core of criminals. When national figures are analysed the proportion of Black and White young males between the ages of 16 and 23 who are involved in muggings is comparable to their proportion in the society.

But Sir Paul made one other fundamental blunder. The date chosen for the meeting was July 28, the anniversary of the death of Joy Gardner, the illegal immigrant who died while being arrested for deportation. The community was still seething at the acquittal of the three officers who were tried for causing her death.

An equally important issue faces the police force. It is the issue of retention. Keeping those Black officers who join the force. The turnover of Black officers is too great. During 1995 the Metropolitan Police Force settled 15 race discrimination cases out of court. This allowed the Met in most cases to pay out some money, avoid a finding against them and for everybody to proceed as if nothing had happened. Indeed Mike Bennett, Chairman of the London branch of the Police Federation which backed one of the applicants before the tribunal, denied that the out-of-court settlement showed that racism persisted in the Met. He did go on to add, however, "There is a recognition today that we have not been fair to Black and female officers."[11]

A suggestion that in future the officers involved might be called upon to meet all or part of the settlement out of their own pockets as a means of bringing some sense of reality to the situation was countered by the Police Federation seeking to arrange special insurance cover for their members. It is regrettable that internal police procedures do not seem capable of providing resolutions to complaints from Black officers ranging from abuse and harassment to unfairness in annual appraisals and failure to achieve hard fought for promotion. The Chief Inspector of Constabulary, Trevor Morris, has accepted that there are still some police officers who treat racism as a joke and consider racist and sexist banter as acceptable and are willing to dismiss any attempts to change attitudes as an act of "political correctness". What is sad is that in many cases, when supervisory officers are confronted with instances of prejudice, harassment and racist exchanges they do nothing about it, thus reinforcing the atmosphere of indifference.

The police force must begin to realise that equal opportunities are crucial to its ability to deliver a quality service. Indeed Trevor Morris (1992) reaffirmed his belief that if the service cannot treat its own staff well it would be difficult if not impossible to demonstrate that members of the public are treated fairly. This is an argument that activists in the Black community have made time and time again and it is encouraging to have it underpinned by the Chief Inspector of Constabulary.

The latest report of the Inspectorate (1996) following the inspection of 13 police forces recognised that substantial progress had been made since the 1992 report but still found unacceptable levels of discrimination. It declared that in some areas the force contained reactionary and prejudiced White men. The report describes scepticism, tokenism and down right indifference and talked about a male "canteen culture" being the order of the day. In many instances it took a high profile legal case against the police service to generate any movement at all.

The report said that there was evidence of continuing high levels of racist banter, perhaps more covert and subtle than before but no less destructive. Racism often went unchallenged by colleagues and senior officers. It also said that while attempts were being made to establish better equal opportunities, these were hindered by entrenched attitudes which continued to frustrate and dilute their best efforts.

The thirteen forces that formed the basis of the report were West Midlands, Greater Manchester, Bedfordshire, Devon and Cornwall, Cambridgeshire, Hertfordshire, Kent, Lincolnshire, Northumbria, North Wales, South Yorkshire, Surrey and Wiltshire.

In 1978 the total police establishment in England and Wales was 90,352 of whom 218 (0.24%) were from ethnic minority groups. By 1995 the total police establishment had risen to 124,000 of whom 2108 (1.7%) were from ethnic minority groups. However the ethnic minority groups make up 5.2% of the economically active population in England and Wales and if this were transferred into the police force we would be expecting to see something in order of 6478 police of ethnic minority origin. This is a national deficit of 4340. But allowing for natural wastage the police forces in England and Wales would have to set a national target to say 500 new Black police per year for ten years. Are they prepared to face up to that challenge. We shall see.

The Metropolitan Police force has launched a scheme first recommended to both the Met and the West Midland Police forces by Community Roots College, a Black led adult training institution some ten years earlier. The programme piloted in the London Borough of Haringey involved targeting the dole queue and encouraging jobless Blacks to sign up to a ten week course to be run jointly with the Industrial Society. The course is designed to help recruits prepare to meet the demands of the forces' selection process. The Met contributed to the financial cost of running the scheme. Participants were able to continue to claim benefits during the period of the course.

Conservative MP for Ryedale John Greenway, himself a former police officer supported the scheme but added:

"I think it right to help the jobless young in Haringey but we should do the same for Asians and Whites in their unemployment blackspots. I think it would be a good idea if the Army also helped to inspire new recruits this way."[12]

Labour MP for Tottenham, Bernie Grant, also gave his support to the scheme. In fact he had been pushing the idea for quite a while. His office issued a supporting statement:

"Black people should be recruited in large groups to provide support for each other in a climate of racism. It is hard for Black people to survive on their own in the police force when they are faced with prejudice. That is why so many are put off the idea altogether or drop

77

out early on. A similar scheme proved quite positive in America, but of course the success of a programme over here depends a great deal on the goodwill of the police."[13]

But as evidence of the level of suspicion the police have to overcome, the scheme did not receive universal approval. Marc Wadsworth of the Anti-racist Alliance said that the police service was not a fit profession for Black people and criticised the initiative. He added:

"The only way to boost the number of Blacks" 'in the force is to rid it of racism first. This plan won't solve the problem. I am in favour of positive action employment schemes, but I make an exception for the police force."[14]

An extensive report on policing in London prepared by the Policy Studies Institute (PSI) and published in 1985 concluded that 63 per cent of young African-Caribbeans were likely to be stopped and searched by police compared with 44 per cent of Whites. It also showed that while a higher proportion of Blacks were taken into custody more were acquitted than Whites. The PSI report observed:

"Every police officer must constantly make decisions about which particular offences he should do something about. The way in which these decisions are taken is of paramount importance."

The Metropolitan Police Commissioner, Sir Paul Condon, addressing a meeting of over 300 people in Lambeth made two significant concessions:

"There are obviously police who are racist. I have no doubt about that" and *"too many Black men are stopped and searched without cause."*[15]

THE COURTS
The next stop in the Criminal Justice System is the courts. It is not the intention to describe here the several different courts and their functions. We are concerned here with the criminal courts and the outcomes of their sentencing function. While the sentencing outcomes tend to vary with different courts, a few general trends seem to emerge.

(a) Nationally, a smaller proportion of Black offenders receive probation and community service orders than White offenders

(b) Black people are disproportionately represented in the prison population compared with White people.

Both of those trends result from the decisions of sentencers.

We have seen how policing has lead to the targeting of Black people for certain types of offences. Studies by the CRE in 1985 carried out in Hackney and by the South East London Probation Service the same year in Croydon support the concept of differential sentencing outcomes. Black young people, even with fewer previous convictions were nearly twice as likely to receive custodial sentences than their White counterparts.

Prison statistics for England and Wales in 1990 showed that 5.8 of the national population comprised of 1.1% African-Caribbean, 2.5% Asian and 2.2% other ethnic minorities group produced 18.2% of the prison population made up by 11.2% African-Caribbean, 2.9% Asian and 4.1% other ethnic minorities groups. In other words a person of African-Caribbean origin was ten times more likely to end up in prison than any other racial group.

When we examine the remand prison population we find that in 1990, the ethnic composition made up 19.7% comprised of 11.8% African-Caribbean. 2.5% Asian and 5.3% other ethnic groups. The over representation in the remand population represents a failure to obtain bail.

It is important to note that when African-Caribbean men are compared in their groupings of young offenders and adult offenders there is a marked differential in custodial sentencing. Of the young offenders 7.9% are African-Caribbean while of the adult offenders 11% are African-Caribbean.

Black young offenders were more likely to be sentenced to prison for robbery (26%) when compared with Whites (12%). The figures were almost reversed when we looked at the proportions sentenced for burglary, 29% being White and 12% Black.

Looking at Black adult offenders, 26% compared with 7% White adult offenders are sentenced for drug offences. For burglary the sentencing outcomes are 7% Black and 17% White while for violence and sex offences there are 27% "Black and 35% White". Those who are not sentenced to prison are dealt with in the community either through fines or one of the various forms of orders supervised by the probation service. Even those sentenced to prison terms will at some stage gain release and be supervised by or need the assistance of the probation service.

Getting the sentencers to admit to any possibility of bias has been an uphill battle. The mere suggestion that it could exist invariably produced a state of involuntary mental rigor mortis in which all reason and rationality got suspended. We are all familiar with the adage that "justice must not only be done, it must be seen to be done" but the British justice system is so steeped in its self-righteousness that it has assumed its fairness to be unassailable. At last however the weight of statistical evidence has begun to bear results.

Justice Brooke has been put in charge of developing race awareness training for judges. The Lord Chancellor has advocated similar training for magistrates and the beginnings have been made in trying to increase the number of Black people involved as sentencers at all levels.

Few Black people sit on advisory committees and are therefore seldom represented in the selection process in the appointment of magistrates. Since 1992 the process has become a little more transparent with the publication of the names of persons sitting on advisory committees. In their book, Black Magistrates, Michael King and Colin May, argue for increasing the number of Black magistrates and stress their role in ensuring justice. They comment however that "there is evidence of racial prejudice among some members of the advisory committees".

A significant contribution to the understanding of how racial discrimination affects the Criminal Justice System was made by a study of crown court sentencing in the West Midlands. The study was undertaken by Dr Roger Hood and Grace Cordovil for the Commission for Racial Equality and was published in 1992. It was based on cases tried at Crown Courts in the West Midlands in Birmingham, Dudley, Coventry, Warwich and Stafford during 1989.

The study afforded comparisons between Whites and the main ethnic minority groups Black, mainly West Indian and Asians, largely of Indian Sub continent origins. The study group were as set out in the following table:

TABLE 12. Number involved in Crown Court study by gender and ethnic group

	White	Black	Asian	Total
Males	1443	889	536	2868
Females	343	776	12	433
Total	1786	965	550	3301

Hood and Cordovil came to the conclusion that 80% of the over representation of Black men in the prison population was accounted for "by the number appearing at Crown Court for sentence and the nature of the characteristic of the cases they were convicted of." They concluded however that the remaining "20% can be attributed to subsequent different treatment."[16] In short as many as one in five sentencing decisions affecting Black people is tainted with discrimination.

THE LEGAL PROFESSION

Both the Law Society and the Bar Council have in recent years come to terms with the need to look seriously at the issue of race as it affected the two bodies. There are a number of common concerns which both bodies have approached with varying degrees of commitment. There are training, access to chamber, distribution of briefs, treatment of Black professionals in court, and commitment to the Black client's case

The Bar Council has an established equal opportunity policy, and is actively pursuing a programme of implementation. The Courts and Legal Services Act 1990 outlawed discrimination on the grounds of race or gender and sections of the Act brought the Bar within the scope of both the Sex Discrimination Act 1975 and the Race Relations Act of 1976.

A survey carried out by the Bar Council in 1989 recalled that 6% of barristers, 10% of new tenants and 12% of all pupils were of ethnic minority groups. One third of all ethnic minority barristers were located in 6 sets of Chambers in London.[17] The Council has developed a comprehensive Equality Code for the Bar.

In October 1994 the Bar Council joined with the Law Society in sponsoring a Conference for lawyers, pupils, trainers and students on how lawyers should respond. In November 1995 with the assistance of the Society of Black Lawyers, the Society of Asian Lawyers and the African, Caribbean and Asian Lawyers Group, the Bar Council together with the Law Society and the Lord Chancellor's Department held a seminar on judicial and silk appointments. Of the 5000 or so judicial appointments just under 2% are held by people of Black ethnic origins.

Considering the past experience of many Black people it is understandable that they harbour suspicions about the level of commitment White solicitors and barristers have in pursuing justice on their behalf. The courts are in themselves an austere and foreboding environment. In a society where justice can still be bought not-with-standing the legal aid scheme, when you have to pay for your legal representation you get what you can afford. Does your advocate think you are worth fighting for? Time and again Black people leave the courts convinced that the person representing them had not really fought for them.

But getting Black lawyers will not necessarily produce any better outcomes. Peter Herbert of the Society of Black Lawyers had this to say:

"The Judiciary tends to patronise Black lawyers and underestimate their ability, and it is up to you to combat that inference and prove yourself. This kind of disrespect for the professionalism of Black people is a deep part of White psychology."

Peter Herbert also argues that there is an unwillingness to accept what

81

is being said by Black people even when they are quoting or presenting information or data assembled by White institutions. He recalls citing the NACRO report on the differential treatment of Blacks and Whites 40 times. Once at Kingston Crown Court he was threatened with disciplinary action and on another occasion he was accused of being political.

THE PRISON SERVICE

The Prison Service quite rightly says that it is not responsible for the number of Black people found in the prisons. They had no part in sending them there. The Service is however responsible for their treatment and well being once they have been admitted to prison. Since 1983 the Prison Service has had a formal race relations policy.

The policy states: "Race relations concerns every member of the Prison Service. It is the responsibility of every member of staff to ensure that the Department's policy is carried out in relation to other members of staff as well as prisoners". The policy is backed up by a detailed manual. However, a recent Home Office study carried out by the Oxford University Centre for Criminological Research revealed that three-quarters of the staff had not read the manual.

The Home Office had commissioned the study to find out the reasons for the differences that seemed to exist between the reported levels of racial attacks and harassment within the prison and those being reported in the world outside. Over the decade of the eighties there had been a steady increase in the number of racist attacks across Britain yet the entire Prison Service only recorded 22 incidents in the whole of 1991.

The study covered interviews with 501 inmates in eight prisons. Of these 128 were White, 220 African-Caribbean, 75 Asian and 78 were from other ethnic groups. Over 180 prison staff were interviewed. Staff were less likely to interpret incidents as being racially motivated than inmates were.

More than a half of African Caribbean inmates, a third of Asian and a quarter of other ethnic minority groups recorded some form of racial abuse, verbal or physical, and or harassment at the hands of prison staff or fellow inmates. Some African-Caribbean inmates claimed to have suffered as many as seven incidents during a three month period prior to talking to the researchers.

The inmates had shown a marked reluctance to use the formal complaints procedure because of a lack of confidence in it and because they feared to use it might get them categorised as "trouble makers" by the staff and might have an effect on their behaviour record and consequently on their release date. This meant that they often bore the abuse in silence.

Black inmates believe that a number of prison staff are either paid up members of the National Front or the British National Party or are sympathisers of those groups. As the Conservative Government pushes ahead with privatisation of prisons this situation is likely to become worse.

Labour MP for Tottenham, Bernie Grant, while welcoming the Home Office Report lamented that the Prison Service was refusing to take the issue seriously and added:

"Racism in prisons takes many forms, and the Prison Service to date has hardly scratched the surface in attempting to deal with it. There are real fears as to how it will be handled in privately run prisons. Dealing with racism takes time and money. Racism on the part of a prison officer must be made a dismissable offence. Every single officer and manager must undertake training in race awareness before being allowed to serve in our jails. More importantly, steps must be taken immediately to change the culture which makes racism so acceptable inside."[18]

While the Courts are responsible for the sentences passed on offenders the prison service has the responsibility for allocating the prisoners. The type of offence committed and the length of sentence to be served do form part of the assessment undertaken in determining the prison at which an inmate serves his/her sentence. This does not fully explain why in 1990 16% of African-Caribbean adults served their sentences in category B closed prisons compared with 11% for all ethnic groups.

The Prison Service demonstrates that policies alone will not meet the needs of Black people. As a Service they have done well at top level and in creating national frameworks. There is a clear equal opportunities statement, training provided for management, a fairly comprehensive data collecting system and a race relations committee in every prison. But it is implementing all this to ensure that the principles reach down to day-to-day activity and become part of the Black prisoner's experience which is much more difficult.

THE PROBATION SERVICE

Any examination of the work of the Probation Service as it affects the lives and prospects of Black people must begin by understanding its position in the Criminal Justice System. The principal focus of the Probation Service is the courts. Probation officers are in fact officers of the court. Any suggestions that they were anything else were dispelled by the Criminal Justice Act 1991, (CJA), which spelt out quite specifically a number of statutory duties.

They are required to write pre-sentence reports which present options available to the court in individual cases. They supervise a range of community sentences imposed by the courts including that part of custodial sentences that are served in the community under the arrangements which the Act makes for various forms of release.

The first set of statistics required under the CJA 1991 are now beginning to come through and their use will determine how effective services will become in their response to the needs of the Black people they serve. By the mid eighties most probation services had formulated race equality policies and had started some crude racial data collecting. As the nineties began, managements were being driven by cash limits to question the benefits of the race equality policies they had put in place.

Since so much of race equality work had been spearheaded by employment issues it is not surprising that services had made great play of their recruitment of Black staff. But nationally there still remains a gross under-representation of Black staff throughout the service. Some of those services which have recruited Black staff have often done so for the wrong reasons. Once they have recruited them, they were ill-prepared to make effective use of their talents or to provide support and open access to career development.

Because of the links the services have with the Diploma in Social Work (Dip.SW) (Probation Option) courses at the various universities they have been able up to now to influence the access of Black people into the profession. Michael Howard, the current Home Secretary, has however dropped the DipSW as being essential to practice as a probation officer. The last supported Home Office course being those who entered training in September 1995. The Home Secretary does not see probation officers as social workers but as prison officers operating in the community rather than in a residential control institution.

This change is bound to have an effect on the entrance of Black people into the Service. If this fear is realised then the Service is likely to face a very severe image crisis. It is not yet certain how in-service training will meet the gap created by the dropping of the DipSW requirement nor how services will respond to the Home Office preference for the recruitment of ex-army personnel available as a result of cuts in the armed forces.

A major function of the probation service is to provide pre-sentence reports for the courts. As part of their anti-racist strategies most services have concentrated on this part of their work. It has attracted the greatest scrutiny as well as produced some of the most heated debate internally. This is a central piece of interaction between the service and its Black clients. It demands a high level of cross cultural communication and a degree of professional self-confidence greater than that required when operating in a homogeneously ethno-centric environment.

84

The main objective here has been to ensure that pre-sentence reports avoid use of stereotypes which are likely to reinforce or awaken prejudices against the subject of the report when the report is submitted to the court. A second objective is that the report covers all appropriate options when drawing up recommendations and does not restrict the options conveyed to the bench.

Services have responded to this challenge in a variety of ways. Some have used gatekeeping, a system whereby officers double check each other on those two objectives. Others have so sanitised their reports that nothing about race ever appears even though to do that may represent a flagrant denial of an essential part of the offender's experience. Yet others offer Black clients the option of having a Black officer prepare their pre-sentence reports. This last option is often taken without reference to the hidden messages it sends out about White and Black officers and the integrity of the service itself.

Many White probation officers have poor links with the Black community, and do not feel that they have been adequately trained to work effectively with Black people. Black officers feel that the service having employed them does not fully appreciate and value them and that they have not been fully integrated into the fabric of the organisation.

Most probation services have adopted policies in relation to anti-racist practice. In general, they seek to offer Black people fair treatment and equal access to all their facilities. The probation service provides a wide range of supervisory activities for those persons whom the courts refer to them. The fact that they do not always succeed in their efforts should not prevent us from acknowledging the amount of time and energy many of them expend in the quest of providing an equitable service to all their clients.

Too often the policies have been driven by activists rather than professional consensus. In many services there is a lack of clarity in respect of the issues and confusion surrounding the terminology in general currency which had given rise to policies being very badly applied in practice. Complaints procedures are generally defective in the area of race equality because of the emotional tension with which they so frequently become embroiled.

As the last stop in the Criminal Justice System, it is important that they are able to use their influence effectively in any inter-agency dialogue between the various parts of the justice system. This will only be possible if they redouble their own efforts to make sense of their endeavours to develop effective anti-racist strategies.

Some leading media personalities from the ethnic communities: Moira Stuart, Zenab Badawi (and below) Trevor McDonald and Rianna Scipio

"The Open Society will come about when all
decent people both Blacks and Whites, are
galvanised to change the present society."

Whitney Young

CHAPTER SIX

BLACK PEOPLE AND THE MEDIA

RACISM AND THE MASS MEDIA

Stuart Hall argues that a significant part of our everyday knowledge of
the world in which we live and the society that inhabits it comes to us
directly or indirectly through pictures of the world and images of the
people and situations in which they function which are presented to us
by the media. He adds:

*"It isn't simply that we recognise the facts about the social world in
them. It is also that the ways in which these groups and relationships
are represented by the media provide us with categories, images,
models, pigeon-holes - a framework through which we classify the
world, and thereby understand it. The media is massively concentrated
and an immensely powerful source of our everyday social knowledge."[1]*

But what the people in the media select for presentation to us is
conditioned by their own past experiences, and unresolved prejudices,
current goals and objectives. To what extent are they merely informing
as opposed to engineering? Do they seek to be agents of change or
merely reinforcing established ideologies? Perhaps they are doing all of
these. What this does mean is that we have constantly to be assessing
and reassessing their outputs to determine what our appropriate
response ought to be.

There are numerous negative stereotypes of Black people still in
existence. That underlying image of inferiority is still there. We may
have moved on from the days when Edward Long author of "A History
of Jamaica" wrote:

*"Three ranks of men (White, Mulatto and Black), dependent on each
other, and rising in a proper climax of sub-ordination, in which the
Whites hold the highest place."*

How much of what now appears in the media is a revamping of Edward Long? Are Black people still being portrayed through the eyes of White supremacists who are conditioned to long past historical caricatures of Black people, and have some Black people so internalised these images that they have lost pride in themselves and become paranoid in their responses to real life?

Indeed Hall argues that we are never free from the images of slavery. The slave had to be strong and obedient on the one hand but primitive; never far removed from savagery and capable of turning against his master. He was never really deserving of complete trust. Nearly fifty years after the wind of change started moving through Africa, Black leaders are still portrayed as unpredictable almost to the point of being primitive. The concept of the Third World (no one knows what happened to the second World) have given way to the developing world useful only as a market for exploitation. When the media portrays the savagery of the Black tribal (primitive) despots, it does not tell us that it was the White west who financed and supplied both sides of the conflict. The interests of the so called civilised world are centred more in the sale of weapons of destruction than in the emergence of a competitive African economy. War and strife in Africa will ensure its continued weakness.

Because of its linkage to the racist ideology, the media fails to unravel the realities of the plight of Africa and hence of Black people throughout the world. For therein lies the image of all Black people. And this continues to happen despite the media's declared intentions to expose racism and to support efforts to eliminate racism in our society.

Civil wars are horrible experiences wherever they take place. The wars in Rwanda and the Balkans were occurring at the same time. Each represented the wanton waste of life and national heritage. One was presented as the savage primitive exercise of uncivilised people, the other the disgraceful episode of ethnic cleansing, a shame on the good name of the European. On the one hand the subscript was one of pity, what does one expect of these poor savages we had not yet been able to bring into the twentieth century and the twenty first approaches. On the other, we coined the rather sophisticated phrase "ethnic cleansing". There was anger and frustration that an area steeped in culture, architecture and art was being indiscriminately destroyed. This was a cause for shame because these people should know better.

But depending too strongly on interpretation of imagery has its dangers. Both White people's perception of Black people and Blac people's perception of themselves is undergoing change and much of the change taking place challenges the old stereotypes. As Black people become more confident of themselves and their achievements, and as most of them join the ranks of producers within the media and bring their own interpretation of the world to bear on the presentation of that world, the nearer we will come to eliminating racism from the media.

POLITICS, RACE AND THE MEDIA

We have seen how the mass media has been instrumental in conveying images and reinforcing ideological concepts. It is equally powerful in articulating political swings. Ian Taylor and Alan Clarke looked at the way in which Law and Order Politics were treated on Television during the 1979 General Election.[2] The events which occurred in Southall on 23 April 1979 were portrayed as a "riot" and thus facilitated a link to be made between legitimate anti-racist protest and the law and order issues naturally associated with riots.

Every election period witnesses a heightening of the debate around immigration. Politicians ruthlessly exploit the facilities of the media to feed fear and anxiety about the threat posed by illegal immigrants. Sadly all political parties have to a greater or lesser extent used the race card during election times to the delight of the media. Each party in turn blaming the others with the media aiding and abetting. It is the time which the media seems unable to resist. Its alibi that it is merely reporting is just not good enough.

Margaret Thatcher achieved a fundamental shift to the right in British politics and John Major despite his stated objectives of seeking to create a classless society has not been able to stem that tide. Tony Blair has taken New Labour into the centre ground previously dominated by one nation Toryism. The treatment of race in the media has been affected adversely as the media has sought to adjust to the more right wing environment.

One significant consequence of this shift has been the way in which the media has picked up and marketed the concept of political correctness. Any anti-racist strategy demanding a measure of societal change is held up to ridicule as political correctness. It would be a miracle if the advocates of equal opportunities never made a mistake and it is true that sometimes some of them are carried away on their own zeal. But the way in which sections of the media treat these lapses reflects their political loyalties.

It is interesting that the dismissive charge of political correctness is on the whole attributed to White people and their institutions seeking to develop anti racist practices, yet when Black people struggle to promote similar practices, they are labelled as being radical or militant. This is largely because Black people are not generally perceived as being able to take any active part in political thinking.

In a democracy we depend on a free press to assist in the upholding of our civil liberties and safeguarding our human rights. We talk of the free press, because unlike radio and television you do not need a licence

89

to run a newspaper. Unfortunately you need money and the majority of people with money happen to be allied to right wing causes or the pursuit of more money or both. In such an environment, race equality takes a low priority. You only need to read some of the tabloids to get a political lesson on the place of Black people in British society.

ADVERTISING

Much of the media is supported by advertising revenue. There is a correlation between distribution levels and the quantity of advertising any part of the media can command. It is important that advertising does not offend and that in the effort to gain support for particular goals it does not reinforce stereotypes.

Look at those appealing letters that come through your letter boxes from Christian-Aid, Save the Children, Oxfam to name but three, and the countless advertisements that appear in our newspapers and on our TV screens. What is common is that they convey one overriding impression of Black children, that of suffering victims. We see them as victims of natural disasters - earthquakes, hurricanes, cyclones, famine or man-made disasters - tribal conflict, civil war, invasion. Each picture in each advertisement is not the centre or focus of our attention. He or she is the example of thousands more poor, sick, emaciated victims of a poor, helpless people - and they are Black.

It says something about our society that in order to tug at our heart strings and to evoke a sense of guilt at the relative plenty we enjoy, advertisers feel compelled to resort to these shock tactics.

There is another type of advertising which calls for attention. It is that which seeks to declare an intention to discriminate. Under Section 29 of the Race Relations Act 1976 it is unlawful to publish an advertisement which indicates or might reasonably be understood to indicate, an intention to discriminate. Proceeding in respect of such advertisements can only be brought by the Commission for Racial Equality.

Each year the Commission handles between 250 and 300 enquiries from the public. The majority of these deal with the legality of particular advertisements in the area of positive action or in respect of the section dealing with genuine occupational qualification. Section 38(1)(b) enables employers to encourage applications from members of racial groups under-represented in their workforce. Section 5(2)(d) enables employers to appoint persons of particular racial groups to posts providing personal services for people from that racial group.

Both employers and publishers have sought the Commission's advice and by that means have been able to get clarification on the limits of the law before proceeding with the advertisements. It is the area of the law which is monitored must closely by opponents of the legislation and the

Commission received about 60-70 complaints every year up to the early 1990's. Since the provisions were more generally used by local authorities and voluntary organisations, there have been fewer advertisements in the last two years as cuts have meant less recruitment overall.

A new form of product advertising by large multi-national companies is conducted through programme sponsorship. The Brewers, Heineken, recently ran into a race row when one of their executives wrote to Planet 24 TV company, whose music show Hotel Babylon was being sponsored by Heineken complaining that there were "too many Negroes in the show and that more 'normal' people should be in the audience". With an eye to business, the company promptly apologised and reprimanded the executive.

COMPLAINTS

Following the Calcutt Committee report, (1990) the Press Council was stood down and in its place a new voluntary body was set up,. It is known as the Press Complaints Commission. The new Code of practice agreed with the Commission by the newspaper and magazine industry contains a clause which sets the standard for reporting on issues of race. Clause 14 says:

(i) The press should avoid prejudicial or pejorative reference to a person's race, colour, religion, sex or sexual orientation or to any physical or mental fitness or handicap.

(ii) It should avoid publishing details of a person's race, colour, religion, sex or sexual orientation, unless these are directly relevant to the story.

Several complaints are received each year alleging various types of references to race in newspapers which the readers feel to be biased. In the majority of complaints which go to adjudication, the majority are upheld. In the first of two cases which, were heard by the old Press Council, a national daily columnist's had described a man awaiting trial for murder as a "black bastard." The Council ruled that the paper had made a "gross and deliberate breach of the repeated ruling against prejudicial references to race or colour unless relevant to the story." Here was a man who had pleaded guilty, was already in custody so no one was looking for him. to introduce colour and race into the story was therefore unnecessary. To link the introduction to a term of abuse was indefensible. In the second case a Sunday newspaper was ruled against for using the term "dago" which was deemed to be a derogatory term of racial abuse.

TRAINING

It has been recognised for a long time that one strategy in seeking to improve the way in which issues of race are treated in the media would be to enhance the number of Black people who enter the journalistic professions. Support for various training initiatives was therefore important. In addition to the BBC programme of training for Black ethnic minority people a number of other schemes exist.

Since 1987 with support from the Commission for Racial Equality, the Vauxhall College of Building and Further Education began an access course for entry to training colleges in journalism. The Polytechnic of Central London (now the University of Westminster) runs a radio journalism course for ethnic minority students and the George Viner Memorial Fund set up in 1988 by the NUJ provides sponsorship for ethnic minority students for training in journalism. The George Viner Memorial Fund also administers the Felix Dearden Memorial Prize. One or more awards are made each year to ethnic minority students on courses recognised by the media industry.

Results from these training initiatives are already starting to come through as the successful students take their place in the world of work. Some have gone to work in the national media, others to local or specialised media and some have gone to strengthen the ethnic media itself. What is evident is that we are seeing a greater involvement in the media than we did a decade ago and the treatment of many issues is becoming more informed. While there is still some distance to go, the journey has begun.

THE BLACK MEDIA

In June 1990 the Commission for Racial Equality held a conference at the TUC National Education Centre in North London to explore the implications of the Broadcasting Bill which was then going through Parliament. It was important to understand how the Broadcasting Act 1990 and the new Radio Authority would affect the access to radio provision for black people.

One participant at the conference made a succinct analysis.

"Black people wish to see a more diverse, more representative and more accountable broadcasting system, which respects the rights, and reflects the interests of all citizens, including those who work in the industry."[3]

It was clear from the outset that a predominantly commercial system could not provide equitable access to the airwaves for smaller disadvantaged groups. While on the one hand Britain likes to claim that it is a multi-cultural society fully respecting the best of the pluralist conventions, it has not accepted as some European countries have, that broadcasting is an essential part of the multi-cultural spectrum and as such is a legitimate focus of official recognition and where appropriate public subsidy.

While some have argued that ethnic programmes which occurred in mainstream broadcasting were often poorly funded, poorly produced and often poorly presented, the resulting response of cutting most ethnic programmes from mainstream and restricting them to local programmes and independent radio has meant that in the largely commercial environment African-Caribbean information and interests have suffered relatively to those minority groups with a stronger communal economic base. A further consequence has been that by and large the new ethnic stations have been unable to invest in grassroots issues and have reflected the concerns of the more established elements of their respective communities.

Those who argue for public subsidy in order to allow the stations to address community concerns fail to grasp the fact that the issues that rate highest on Black people's list of concerns are the most likely to be the very issues that governments of all persuasions have tried to ensure never get a public airing. Governments have always tried to keep control of the Black debate. Imagine full blooded Black debate on radio on such topics as police community relations, racial harassment, and discrimination in the criminal justice system; to mention but three. Rather than face the prospect of having to withdraw the subsidy, governments are happy to pass the control to market forces and let programmes be determined by what advertisers and sponsors are prepared to support.

Clause 89 of the Broadcasting Act 1990 insists that Independent Radio services must present news accurately and impartially. It demands that programmes must not give undue prominence to the news and opinions of particular persons or bodies on matters of current political or industrial controversy or current public policy nor may the views and opinions of those persons providing the service be expressed on these matters.

The Broadcasting Act of 1981 laid down in very specific terms what was expected of stations by way of their programme strategy, It said that:

"...the programmes broadcast from any station or stations contain a suitable proportion of matter calculated to appeal specially to the taste and outlook of persons served by the station or stations and, where another language as well as English is in common use among those so served, a suitable proportion of matter in that language."

93

The BBC continues to provide through its regional radio a number of programmes specifically geared to ethnic and linguistic minorities. As the major public service institution it would be a dereliction of duty if the emergence of local commercial radio allowed the BBC to reduce its ethnic minority programming. The BBC has been slowly developing its equal opportunities policy within network radio and this is geared towards affecting programmes as well as professional staffing where the BBC has a target of 8% by the year 2000. In 1989 the ethnic minority proportion of the professional staff was 4%.

The oldest independent local community stations are now well established. They have tested out the boundaries and discovered what is possible for them within the limitations of financial resources and license restrictions. Sunset Radio serves Manchester; Sunrise Radio covers Ealing, Hounslow and Southall; Radio Harmony supplies Coventry; Spectrum Radio spreads over Greater London with a multi-ethnic menu and Choice FM meets the needs of Brixton, and South London. As we approach the year 2000 more independent community stations will come on stream and the Black community will be expecting to increase its current number of stations building on the experience of its pioneers.

As far as newspapers are concerned the main weekly papers are *Caribbean Times (incorporating African Times)*, *Asian Times* and the *Voice*. The two issues that confront the Black community in ways that no Black newspaper can ignore are immigration and the police. It is how the papers respond to those two issues that will determine their relevance to the community and in the long run their survival.

While the establishment has tended to apply subtle commercial pressures in the past, Sir Paul Condon, Commissioner of the Metropolitan Police, broke that tradition in January 1996 when being interviewed on London News 97.3 FM. He launched a rarely outspoken attack on the *Voice*. The targets in point were stories they had published about the death of Wayne Douglas in police custody and the riots in Brixton which followed a rally in connection with the death. Sir Paul said:

"Sadly, I believe they have been irresponsible, dangerously irresponsible. I think they have fuelled discontent, I think they have printed alleged eye-witness accounts that were never substantiated."[4]

He is also reported as saying:

"They printed allegations which were, I think, unnecessarily inflammatory, that had no substance. I am not prejudging the outcome of an independent inquiry, but, to the best of my knowledge,

the wild allegations that were made have not been substantiated in any way, shape or form at all. I think it is a missed opportunity. It is a tragedy that one of the most important papers in that area chooses an editorial line which I think is dangerously confrontational."

It is to the credit of the *Voice* that Sir Paul unleashed such an attack. If he felt the report was so irresponsible and so likely to fuel discontent, he could have gone to the Press Complaints Commission. When he complained that what the *Voice* wrote was unnecessarily inflammatory was he providing a licence to publish material that was "necessarily'" inflammatory and would those conditions arise?

What the *Voice* had done was to run a story under the headline "Tell us the truth" and under a photograph of four of the new long-handle batons now carried by police was the question, "Did they play a role in Wayne's death?". The reason for this lay in the claim by the *Voice* that they had a sworn affidavit from an eye witness to the events who was ready to go into court to give evidence if necessary. They felt they had a public duty to raise the issues and they rejected Sir Paul's claim of dangerous irresponsibility. Their experience, however, demonstrated the lengths to which the powers-that-be will go once you start to defend the rights and interests of the Black community. In short they are quite prepared to limit the right to free expression when it suits the interests of the establishment.

MEDIA AWARDS

In 1992 the Commission for Racial Equality (CRE) launched the first Race in the Media Award initiative in the UK. This followed a similar scheme that had been running in Holland since 1988. Germany also has a media award for outstanding contribution to a better understanding of race relations. Belgium has a comparable programme.

The CRE is convinced that the Award scheme has made a number of important results in its first four years:

It has raised the profile of ethnic minorities to the reading and listening public.

- It has helped to remove the very narrow focus of ethnic minorities simply being portrayed as the "problem" by giving more informed and balanced coverage of the many aspects of ethnic minority life.

- It has provided a mechanism for formally acknowledging the outstanding contribution of individual journalists and broadcasters toward a better understanding of race issues.

- It has helped to improve the climate for better understanding of race and community relations.

In launching the Scheme, Sir Michael Day, Chairman of the CRE said:

"Sensitive and informed coverage of race issues by the media must be encouraged. This award will give a unique opportunity for journalists and broadcasters to demonstrate how they are contributing to a better understanding of race relations in this country."

The first awards sponsored by Unison were made in seven separate categories. National newspapers; regional and local newspaper; specialist journal/magazine; radio drama; radio current affairs/documentary; TV Drama; TV current affairs/documentary. A new category of multi-media Youth sponsored by MTV(Europe) was introduced in the second year.

For the 1994 awards the radio and TV categories were increased from two to four. Radio news; radio factual; radio entertainment and radio drama; television news; television factual; television entertainment and television drama. This change increased the categories to twelve.

The popularity of the awards has grown over the years. In four short years the number of entries has grown to over 250 a year and the sponsorship of the awards has broadened to include a range of media print and publishing companies.

Some of the winners of the 1994 awards will give some idea of the spread of talent. In the national newspaper category there were joint winners in Vivek Chaudhary of *The Guardian* for his coverage of topical race issues and Prabjot Dolly Dhingra of *The Independent* for her lively arts coverage of cultural aspects of ethnic minority life.

Another joint award was in the specialist magazine/journal category where the joint award went to the *Weekly Journal* for its consistent coverage of race issues, and to freelance journalist, Reva Klein, for her thoughtful and careful writing on race and education for *The Times Educational Supplement.*

In the radio factual category the award went to Euan Meilwraith and Angus Coull, BBC Radio Scotland for an incisive programme on Asian and gypsy communities. Andrew Burroughs BBC TV news won the Television News category and Masterchef, Chef II produced by Crucial Films for BBC1 won the Television Entertainment category.

Maria Williams received the multi-media category Youth, for her series on BBC Radio 1 FM "Listen Without Prejudice".

> "I have cherished the idea of a democratic and free society in which all persons live together in harmony and with equal opportunities"

> Nelson Mandela

CHAPTER SEVEN

THE NEW POLITICS

THE ETHICAL DILEMMAS

In the preface to Charles Taylor's essay "Multiculturalism and the Politics of Recognition" Amy Gutman the Director of University Centre for Human Values at Princeton University poses the question: "Can people who differ in their moral perspectives nonetheless reason together in ways that are productive of the greater ethical understanding?" This is fundamental to making progress in a multicultural, multiracial society. The important issue here is whether or not people are prepared to "reason together".

People on the extremes of politics are very seldom interested in "reasoning together" and because as a matter of principle one ought not to compromise with racism many people find it difficult to enter into dialogue with those whose perspectives they do not share.

Three concepts have come into very frequent use in the new politics. One is the old chestnut of freedom of speech under which the ultra right and sometimes the ultra left feel they can peddle their various forms of racism and hatred under the banner of free speech. While it is important to emphasise the value of free speech, it has to be recognised that the right of free speech carries with it a responsibility to others of the right to respect and the freedom from abuse.

But the issue of freedom of speech enters an even more sensitive area when it embodies the claims made for academic freedom. Christopher Brand, psychology lecturer at Edinburgh University has recently written a book on IQ which has been withdrawn by its publishers. Brand claimed that Black people were less intelligent than White people and that single mothers should be "encouraged to breed with higher IQ males to escape the poverty trap".

The students' Union sought to have him dismissed and the academic staff were divided in what should happen to him. Some of his severest

97

academic critics defended his right to freedom of expression and deplored the censorship implicit in the banning of his book. Brand also advised the Lothian Police on IQ testing for officers and this stirred the Lothian Racial Equality Council to issue a statement through its spokesperson. It said:

"It will undermine the confidence of the ethnic community in the police."

Brand is not alone in maintaining that there is a direct link between IQ and race. A number of American academics, including Roger Pearson assert the same. Pearson has even gone as far as to suggest the creation of a "supergeneration" engineered genetically from the fittest White people.

What has given Brand and his friends and colleagues so much comfort is the fact that while they have heard condemnation and calls for their ostracism, there has been little coherent rebuttal of the theories they propound. Black people will certainly feel aggrieved and if any of them has the misfortune to be taught by him they will surely suspect any grading he gives them. The real question is has Brand compromised his academic integrity?

There is a balance to be preserved, and only through its preservation can the society hope to create a safe environment so necessary to the development of social cohesion. Racial abuse cannot be tolerated under the guise of freedom of speech.

Then there is the issue of choice. The Government has made a lot of the politics of choice. It is forever claiming that it is providing choice to the people. But there is no point in having a theoretical choice of A, B and C if you can only afford A. Hence choice is limited by your ability to exercise it. So that access which governments have so often failed to ensure the Black communities were able to attain becomes crucial to their exercise of choice. Similarly the choice between A, B and C is only valid if one has full information on all three. So the absence of information will affect the different choices people make. In short, there is not genuine choice to all without equality of opportunity in terms of access and information. When one champions choice, how can one be sure one is offering genuine choice?

Finally there is the concept of political correctness. The proponents of change have made a number of recommendations over the years. These have been both linguistic changes and practical changes. Some of these have been well argued and soundly based. Others are less well founded and the opponents of change have seized upon these and sought to demean the whole process and push for change as an exercise in political correctness which has now become a term of derision. So much has the usage of language changed. What is required is a dispassionate dialogue between the opposing views not a dismissive epithet.

MAKING THE LAW EFFECTIVE

We have now had over thirty years of race relations legislation. So far, it has applied only to England, Scotland and Wales. Surely it is time that it is extended to include Northern Ireland. There seems no logical reason why it should not. The last Act is now 20 years old and all would benefit from a thorough review designed to make it more effective.

The Commission for Racial Equality as part of its statutory function has prepared and submitted to Government its own review in 1985. It updated that review in 1991, but Government has not been minded to move constructively in this area.

Despite the growth of racial harassment and anti-Semitism the process of dealing with incitement to racial hatred has become so cumbersome and so few prosecutions have been brought that there is a general loss of confidence in any action being taken. It is doubtful whether racial harassment could have reached its terrifying levels had there not been an underpinning of inflammatory material. An independent review of how incitement to racial hatred is handled is long overdue.

In order to speed up the resolution of discrimination cases and thus strengthen the public's perception of the effectiveness of the law, the creation of a discrimination division in the industrial tribunals has for some time been urged upon Government.

While the increase in the level of the awards which the industrial tribunals have made has been raised substantially, the introduction of class actions would be an even greater spur to the elimination of discrimination. Instead of each individual in a class having to bring a separate litigation, one test case would suffice the establishment of both fact and principle and the result applied to all claims within the class.

A number of local authorities had sought to use their powers under section 71 of the Race Relation Act to seek to use their purchasing power to extend the principle of equality of opportunity by the use of contract compliance procedures. However, rather than welcoming these initiatives, the Government intervened to limit the right of local authorities through section 18 of the Local Government Act 1988. In place of the monitoring data which the authorities were seeking, the Government instituted a set of approved questions which were short on detail and narrow in scope.

What is interesting is that since 1948 most government contracts had an equal opportunity clause. The fact however was that no one monitored the operation. Considering the resistance the Government had to contract compliance in England Scotland and Wales, it was surprising that it included contract compliance provisions in Northern Ireland in 1989 in respect of discrimination in employment. Employers in Ulster are compelled by law to provide religious monitoring data and this has been tied in with their eligibility for public contracts. It is hard to resist the conclusion that the Government gave way to American pressure led by the Irish American lobby and Congress that only in this way would American inward investment be guaranteed.

It may well mean that only when the Black people in Britain are able to establish a functional relationship with the Black Caucus in the American Congress and establish a Pan European Black Alliance that the changes necessary to make the law effective will be achieved. The Commission for Racial Equality has done its job in administering the Act through its first two decades and it has reviewed its functioning and made representations to Government. The Government must now be persuaded to respond.

Michael Day when launching the 1990 Report of the Commission for Racial Equality said:

"We want to see a Race Relations Act that is wider in scope, clearer in its terms, less cumbersome in its application and thereby more effective than the present one. We need to modify the law and respond with imagination, if we are to contain the turbulence which is inevitable within a society and world order as people struggle for their share of power, influence and resources."

But when we consider the role of the law in achieving the elimination of racial discrimination and the promotion of equality of opportunity and good race relations, we are constantly reminded of the words of Lord Diplock in the case of London Borough of Hillingdon vs CRE (1982). He said then:

"Racial discrimination is not normally practised openly. It may take a whole variety of subtle forms that are not easy to uncover."

One missing element in this search for a more effective legislation is the absence of a coherent Black led Civil Rights movement. Government does not perceive itself to be under any political pressure to respond to the Commission's urgings in the absence of a clearly articulated set of demands from the victims of discrimination. Joe Harte, Co-Chairman of Black Rights (UK) summing up their Human Rights and the Media Conference seized the opportunity to announce:

"We intend to transform this organisation into the largest Civil

Rights organisation in this country... and we would like you to join us in full force."

IMMIGRATION AND ASYLUM

Nothing so surely signals the second half of a government's term of office than the raising of the political temperature by the use of the several strands of the race issue. The Tory Party has always held that the best route to a harmonious multiracial society was that of firm control of Immigration. This has allowed them to play upon the fears and prejudices of the majority community at any time that suits them politically.

Every country needs an effective immigration policy both for effective planning and for security reasons. Black people are as aware as anyone else of this necessity; but they expect not only that the policy be fair, but that it is applied fairly. Black criticism of the immigration policy is not an attack on British sovereignty but a challenge to the unfairness and sometimes sheer brutality with which it is implemented.

Not only Black people are deported from Britain. Yet in the majority of cases where tragedies such as the Joy Gardner death occur, where dawn raids are made, and where a plane load of people on a charter flight coming to spend Christmas with their relatives find that half are refused entry, the persons involved are Black. The way in which the Government feeds fear and incites suspicion of Black travellers creates a situation at ports of entry that even when one is carrying a UK passport, immigration officers are likely to challenge its validity.

Airlines can be penalised for carrying passengers who are subsequently not given entry and this converts the airline into acting as unofficial agent of the immigration service if it wishes to ensure it avoids penalty. The Home Office has declared its intention to place a responsibility on employers to ensure that the people they employ are entitled to live and work in Britain. In fact another tier of unpaid immigration officers. Faced with this prospect many employers will take what for them will be the safe route and avoid employing Black people.

Despite appeals from a number of Black and refugee organisations the British Government has refused to join other European Governments as signatories to the Schengen Agreement and abolish document checks for travellers between their respective countries.[1] The UK government maintains its support for the tabloid campaign of fear and hysteria around the issues of "bogus refugees and the threat to Britain from a tide of migrants waiting to flood this country".

The Home Secretary resisted sustained criticism of his Asylum policy. He claimed:

"This country has an honourable record of providing refuge for people escaping persecution. We are determined to maintain that record. But the fact is that the vast majority of those claiming asylum are bogus applicants. In most cases they are really economic migrants seeking a better life than they can find in their own countries."

All 2000 Nigerians who sought asylum in Britain in 1995 had their applications rejected. Not even the world condemned execution of writer and activist Ken Saro-Wiwa in November 1995 caused any change in attitude. Of 720 Nigerians whose applications were considered since the execution, all were rejected. Similarly all Rwandan applicants were rejected as were 91% of those from Sri Lanka. It is apparent that Black applicants are not welcomed with "a humanitarian response but with suspicion and a presumption of guilt", is the considered opinion of Nick Hardwick, Chief Executive of the Refugee Council.[2]

THE EUROPEAN DIMENSION

1992 witnessed the completion of the processes which led to the full realisation of the Single European Market. From that time EC citizens gained the right to work, establish businesses and trade in other EC countries. For Black people who would wish to take advantage of this opportunity it is important for them and their families to assess the advantages and disadvantages of such a step.

All the other European countries have some form of protection against racial discrimination. They provide a variety of instruments, constitutional guarantees, provisions within the criminal codes but none are as over arching and comprehensive as the race relations legislation in Britain. You would not find an equivalent enforcement agency to the Commission for Racial Equality. So that with all its known weaknesses, the overall protection in Britain is greater than in any other part of the European Union.

The European Union law has not developed to provide protection for persons on the grounds of racial discrimination except in the narrow ground of nationality. Issues of race, colour and ethnicity are not covered. It does appear that the Union does have the legal competence and the ability to develop the jurisprudence but so far has not found the political will to do so. The protection from racial discrimination in the European Convention on Human Rights is a subsidiary means of protection and depends on the exercise of other convention rights.

The European Parliament has had reports laid before it in 1985 and 1990. While calls have been made for the review of national legislation against political extremism, racism and racial discrimination[3] there has not been very much action. What all of this means is that if Black people came from another EC country to Britain they immediately acquire the full protection of our anti-discriminatory laws, but if Black people go from Britain to other EC countries they lose the protection of British laws and come under the lesser protection of the country to which they go.

There is also a further and more fundamental danger. There is a process of harmonisation of European laws going on. Will this lead to an improvement in the protection from racial discrimination across Europe, or shall we witness a reduction as Britain trades the protection of Black people for other perceived gains? Has Britain through its opt out of the social chapter weakened its hand in defending the right of Black people seeking free movement in Europe?

It is not only the National Front in France who in the Spring of 1996 is exceeding 20% in the opinion polls, but also the rise of fascist elements throughout Europe that give rise for concern. As unified Germany develops the German-Franco axis of the European Union and Britain dithers on her role and allows her influence to wane, Black people in particular must be wary of their future in Europe. Their gloom probably mirrored those of the inmates of a prison where a notice carried this stark information:

"In the interest of economy the light at the end of the tunnel has been switched off."

THE CASE FOR A BILL OF RIGHTS

There are serious doubts as to whether any European Government is ready to promote a Bill of Rights which would include and protect the rights of their Black citizens. But before we condemn, we need to explore the case for a Bill of Rights. Unlike the USA where the written constitution provides a number of constitutional rights, there is no written constitution in Britain and rights are derived from a body of law and international conventions to which we subscribe.

What this adds up to is a system of jurisprudence combined with a parliamentary democracy which asserts the doctrine of freedom, but which leaves citizens in general and Black citizens in particular very much at the mercy of the political and administrative bureaucracy. Indeed rights are nowhere defined and we do not know where to go to get them defined.

Lord Scarman delivering the Keynote address at the Conference on Black People Human Rights and the Media in November 1988 said:

"Have we then as a people a common understanding of what is meant by Human Rights? Do we regard it as important that we

should observe them? The evidence of what British people do in their daily lives and in their daily politics suggests that we lack that common understanding of what is meant by fundamental rights. We lack the understanding that they are rights to which all mankind is entitled, and that they are rights, as Jefferson said two hundred years ago, which are inalienable, i.e. cannot be divested."[4]

If society is to be spared the tyranny of the majority, then the democratic process must be underpinned by that common understanding of what rights each and every individual is entitled. There is a difference in perception between the Race Relations Act as an expression of social liberalism to a minority in our midst and the corporate societal duty to protect the rights and opportunities of that minority as citizens. For if that protection is not derived as a right, then it must be a favour.

Tony Blair has argued for a stakeholder society and has claimed that he wishes to see a Britain in which rights are balanced with responsibilities. Yet without a clear and common view of what those rights are, citizens will remain confused as to their responsibility. This confusion remains particularly acute for Black people who have found barriers put in their way to access to the professions, access to government service and even access to Parliament itself.

Because Parliament is sovereign, and because there are no inalienable rights, it would be possible for Parliament to rescind any of the existing protection provided to Black citizens, and there would be no remedy against an Act of Parliament, however regressive that Act was. The powers provided to the House of Commons by the Parliament Act 1911 mean that a majority in the House of Commons will carry the day. The Honourable Members of Parliament seldom get the opportunity to exercise a free vote according to their consciences. They are whipped in to vote as their party leadership determines. Where a government enjoys a large majority it can safely ignore the opposition. What we have is an elected government free to act at best as a one party state and at worst as a dictatorship. We have seen both in recent years. We must have a Bill of Rights to ensure good government in the 21st Century.

THE DRIVE FOR POLITICAL RECOGNITION
When Louis Farrakhan organised the Million Man March in Washington in October 1995, The Nation of Islam, led in Britain by Wayne X organised a rally on Broad Water Farm to coincide with the Washington March. The movement advocates Black self help, coupled with self discipline as a route to political recognition. It is gaining ground among the Black unemployed young people. Although linked to

104

a separatist ideology, the movement tries to guide its members away from drugs and crime.

Another strand of Black society is seeking recognition through mainstream politics. The 1992 general election brought the number of Black Members of Parliament up from 4 to 6. The next general election due by the Spring of 1997 for the latest should see this number increased still further but nowhere near the 30-35 that it should be. So far neither of the major parties has taken this issue seriously. They are quite happy to have Black members, but the party leaderships remain terrified of devising positive strategies for ensuring movement in this area.

The Labour Party has opposed the integration of a Black section into the framework of the party's machinery and the Tory Party still has not recovered from the loss of the Cheltenham seat to the Liberal Democratic Party because John Taylor, a Black barrister who had been serving as a political adviser to the Home Secretary, was deserted by sufficient local Tory workers and supporters to lose what would, under normal circumstances, have been considered a safe seat.

Sections of the Muslim community were so frustrated at the way in which the political establishment was denying access to them and marginalising their concerns that they set up the Muslim Parliament. But this exercise has not substantially improved their benefits. It was however, a bold and imaginative initiative which has cemented a sense of purpose and direction for its followers.

When Black people do run for parliament their success rate is broadly in line with White success. There were 22 Black candidates among the almost 2200 put forward by the main parties. Six of these were successful. The problem seems to lie in being selected as a candidate. This fact turns our attention to the breeding grounds for future Members of Parliament. Local councillors, company directors, legal professionals, union officials and journalists are the principal pools from which they are drawn.

In 1995, 360 out of some 23,000 local councillors were Black (1.6 per cent of the total compared with 6.9 of working age British citizens who are Black.)[5] The number of Black people who are directors except in their own companies is statistically insignificant. As we have seen earlier, the number of Black journalists and barristers is improving slowly.

In *The Independent* of 10 October 1995, the editor makes this point:

"Britain is full of barriers to halt the advance of those beyond the pale: schooling, accent, background - and the greatest hurdle, colour - are all used to exclude people from the elite."[6]

We are striving for the British equivalents to General Colin Powell, Supreme Court Justice Clarence Thomas, Secretary of Commerce Ron Brown or Ambassador to the UN Andrew Young.

Notting Hill Carnival

> "The great thing in this world is not so much where
> we are but in what direction we are moving."
>
> Oliver Holmes

CHAPTER EIGHT

THE BLACK AGENDA 2000

THE BASIC PRINCIPLES

As we approach the end of the twentieth century and move forward into the twenty-first century it is of the greatest importance that the Black community in Britain is aware of the direction in which it is moving. We have seen in the preceding chapters how Black Britain has been isolated and disadvantaged. It was Mahatma Gandhi who said "It is better to light a candle than to curse the darkness."

Creating a Black Agenda 2000 is an attempt to heed the Gandhi dictum and light a candle. The principles underpinning the development of this agenda are three. Firstly, the agenda while seeking to come to grips with the disadvantages and discrimination so persistent in Black peoples' lives is conscious of the fact that we share a common humanity and that the policies put forward must have a fundamental fairness about them.

Secondly, the agenda is not restricted to issues of race, but is inclusive of the much wider range of public governance. Black people cannot expect the society to have an interest in them if they do not have an interest in the society. To obtain the fullest benefits, all must participate in the process of societal development. The agenda therefore seeks routes of entrance to areas from which Black people have hitherto been excluded.

Finally, part of the unfairness and inequality in society has resulted from structural and organisational weakness. These will need to be corrected, and agenda 2000 seeks to make a start with the more important of these.

The first steps will involve the coming together of the various Black organisations to forge an alliance. This should not be along political party lines, but along community lines so that people could gain the broadest possible insights into community needs and concerns and how these relate to the wider community. The alliance should largely be an educative and supportive mechanism. It should provide the focal point for determining areas for research, setting the terms of reference for such activity and the evaluation and dissemination of the results.

THE ECONOMIC AGENDA
Black people have suffered severely and disproportionately from the Government's strategy of seeking to control the unions through a mix of legislative instruments and the rather crude device of high unemployment and a squeeze on public sector pay. The Black community must argue for higher levels of employment and for a programme designed to cut the level of unemployment in the Black community to the level of employment in the society as a whole within the decade ending in 2006. It must also seek a level of average pay for Black workers in line with average pay nationally. To achieve this, they will need to support efforts to achieve minimum pay levels by statutory means if necessary.

In the last decade, more and more women have been drafted into the workforce. Because a high number of Black women workers are also single parents the community will need to be pressing strongly for workplace crÊches or a child care voucher system. Black women have to be rescued from the part-time, low pay, ununionised environment in which so many of them have found themselves.

Black people know all too well the consequences of high inflation, but they also know the trauma of unemployment. While they argue for control of inflation, they must campaign for jobs. For many this may mean retraining. The days of spending ones entire working life in one job are now largely past. Three is the current average and it is gradually going up.

Black people must push to be included not only as recipients but also as providers of any skills development programmes, linked to local needs, which are developed. The success of any economy depends on the productive skills of its people and its ability to use all its talents. Black people must enter wholeheartedly into all the training opportunities that present themselves. They will often have to achieve these goals in spite of an institutionalised system of discrimination. A collective approach will none the less prove advantageous in making progress.

PRIVATISATION
The Conservative Government has turned the process of privatisation into a form of political correctness. We have seen that privatisation does not necessarily yield efficiency. Efficiency is not a function of ownership but of management. Nor indeed is it necessary to have competition in order to be efficient. To break up a natural monopoly

in order to achieve a spurious competition far from being efficient is wasteful. There is no right way of doing the wrong thing, and in many instances privatisation is simply wrong.

It may be too late and surely too costly to re-nationalise many, if any, of those public sector industries that have been privatised over the Thatcher-Major premierships. However we should ensure that they do not become swallowed up by powerful multi- nationals who are clearly uncontrollable by national governments and who are likely to abuse their market position.

The Black community must therefore argue for stronger powers for the watchdogs of the privatised industries. They should ensure that efficiency is balanced with effectiveness, cost efficiency with quality and managerial expediency with customer satisfaction. Competitiveness ought not to be sought at the expense of fair pay nor the conditions for workers sacrificed for exorbitant bonuses for top management. The competitive output is achieved as much by the workers as by the skills of the manager. There should be some element of fairness in how these rewards are determined.

A MATTER OF GOVERNMENT

The first past the post system of electing members of the House of Commons while reasonably safe in a two party environment is not adequate to serve a society where there are more than two national political parties. What has happened in the last four elections, and likely to happen in the next if the rules are not changed, is that a minority of the popular vote has produced a majority in parliament who could then proceed as Thatcher did, to govern as an elected dictatorship.

As a matter of equality and fairness Black people should be arguing strongly for proportional representation. A people who have suffered from being excluded and marginalised in society ought to be campaigning strongly for inclusiveness. If Tony Blair's stakeholder society is to mean anything at all, then it must mean the end of the first past the post system which so marginalises the contribution minority groups can make to the governance of society.

Black people should also be proposing a fixed term parliament and bring an end to the phoney war between the government and the opposition which is neither serious polities nor good theatre. A system where MPs have ceased to be representatives of the views and concerns of their constituents and on most occasions appear as voting fodder for their respective front benches is a matter that should be seriously looked at again. The role of select committees should be strengthened as part of the development of greater control over the executive by the House of Commons.

Tony Blair should get the support of Black people in the revision of the House of Lords but they should be pressing all main parties to look at the way in which they select prospective candidates for parliament to ensure that greater access is achieved by Black people, who are underrepresented in both houses of parliament.

While the Industrial Tribunal ruled that the women only short list as a means of selecting parliamentary candidates was unlawful, we at least saw a demonstration on the part of the Labour Party to set a target and a time frame in which to achieve it in so far as women were concerned. In the absence of any similar process of target setting, are we to assume that the Party feels at ease with the number of Black people in parliament?

Black people should press home the point that the abolition of the Greater London Council and the six other metropolitan county councils was an act of unpardonable political vandalism. London remains alone among the major capital cities in the democratic world without a democratically elected authority. They should demand that an elected Greater London Authority be re-established.

The Regionalisation of England, each with its own assembly, the Scottish Parliament and assemblies in Wales and Northern Ireland would take the first steps in rolling back the centralisation of Britain. Britain is now the most centralised country in western Europe. It is important that people are made to feel more involved in the decisions which affect their lives and devolved government is the first move in that direction.

DEALING WITH DISCRIMINATION
Most Black people suffer from at least one other form of discrimination in addition to discrimination on the grounds of race. The Commission for Racial Equality has been trying for over a decade to get the Home Office to make certain improvements in the Race Relations Act 1976. The lack of a broad based Black led Civil Rights movement strongly supporting the Commission's case has been a serious handicap which must be rectified.

Equally important is the fact that although the UK government is a signatory to the European Convention on Human Rights the government has not as yet incorporated the convention and its protocols into British law. This should now be done as a matter of urgency through the passing of a Bill of Rights.

Black people should also be pressing for a Freedom of Information Bill. One of the major ways in which Black people have been discriminated against is in the prejudicial information that is held on them and disseminated about them without their knowledge and in the difficulty they have in accessing information to which they are entitled.

Another area of discrimination which needs urgent attention is that of Nationality and Immigration Law. Black people must be assured that Immigration procedures are open and fair. They must be convinced that when they carry a British passport they can expect the same treatment as other British passport holders. Seekers of asylum will want to know that the colour of their skin is not going to prejudice the outcome of their applications.

LAW AND ORDER

Black people are like all other groups in society largely law abiding. They are concerned at the failure to establish an unquestioned total rapport with the police. As a community, they wish to play their full part in the development of an acceptable level of confidence between themselves and the police. The community however has not arrived at a consensus of how this may best be done. However the balance of support in the argument is in favour of seeing the numbers of Black people in the police force increase substantially over the next few years.

They will continue to urge the police forces not only to speed up their recruitment of Black officers, but to look at the ways of ensuring promotion and retention among those they have recruited. They also want to see the police do something about dealing positively with issues of racial abuse and harassment which they see as a major deterrent to progress.

Local community groups must seek to identify and promote Black people in their area who are committed to the criminal justice system and who would be willing to serve as magistrates, probation assistants or prison visitors. The aim being to ensure that there is a constant supply of new people going forward in these areas where at the present time there is great under representation. Another exercise should be focused on young people who have the academic background to pursue a career in the legal profession. Each area should develop its own targets and pursue them assiduously.

EDUCATION AND EMPLOYMENT

The linking of the Department of Education and Science and the Department of Employment into one mega-department should assist in a more coherent response from education to the needs of employment. Black people must now develop a strategy of intervention to secure the interest of their children's education. It is not enough to sit down and complain about the inadequacies of the system.

Those who are qualified to do so must take up the challenge on behalf of the others. The community must set targets and go after

113

them. We are in a new technological age. Those are the skills that employers will demand.

Discrimination in the system has to be fought. We must improve both the quantity and quality of Black teachers in the classroom. Slowly Black teachers are taking charge of inner city schools and more Black people are being appointed as school governors. But the national curriculum has not found a place for multi-cultural studies. The Muslim community has taken the lead in developing and controlling a network of its own schools and this must certainly dominate the agenda for the other ethnic groups. Here is one area in which the competitive environment operates to everyone's benefit. If one community does not secure the interests of its own children - and education is the best form of security - it cannot complain that its children's interests have been neglected by someone else.

The Black community must therefore secure its future by developing a network of educational institutions as models of excellence and thus dispel the myth that their children are intellectually inadequate. This objective more than any other will be resisted by the establishment but the strength of that resistance is but a measure of its importance. It will require the creation of an education or development fund to underpin such a drive.

The successful minority communities have been those which have been able to establish a niche in the market place. Discrimination in employment will not be abandoned until Black people have a larger share of the business market and have created a number of jobs largely equivalent to the number of Black people in the labour force market. It is that equivalency of opportunity that will squeeze discrimination out of the system.

There is urgency attached to the way in which minority Chambers of Commerce are developed and the strength of support and advocacy they can offer to their members. There is also an urgent need to assess the actual economic contribution that Black businesses are making to the gross national product. This is information which the Government doubtlessly has, but the community does not. This must be rectified. It is crucial to have this information as it illustrates the strength of any community's bargaining power when it is seeking to influence policy changes.

The Black community should seek to reduce by 50% the unemployment in its midst within a decade and to ensure that it has strategies in place to prevent it going above the national average. No government could refuse partnership on those terms.

It is very crucial that the Black community through its involvement at all levels of the employment field ensures that employers, trades unions and associated professional bodies all have fully operational equal opportunity policies. The movement of Black people into the boardrooms of the larger companies must be achieved as part of the agenda 2000.

Once again attention must be drawn to the fact that the Government and the major companies did launch an initiative to ensure the advancement of women through what was known as the glass ceiling. While the initiative did not measure up to the fanfare of its launching and with time has lost some of its impetus it did achieve some gains for women which would hardly have been met without it. The Black community must demand that the Government and the major companies make a similar commitment on the issue of employment opportunities for Black people.

The Black community must continue to press for the inclusion of contract compliance clauses in all public sector contracts. It is a public scandal that the Government should use taxes obtained from the sweat of Black people's labours to finance companies who would wilfully exclude Black people from a fair access to their jobs or promotion on equal terms within their organisations. The idea that contract compliance constitutes undue interference in the rights of companies to manage their own affairs must be contested strenuously. It is simply a matter of equity. It is an issue of working to establish social cohesion which is impossible in an unjust society. This is too important for the Black community to let it slide.

HOUSING

Poor housing has been a problem in the Black community from the time they arrived in Britain. Three generations have seen modest improvements and this agenda seeks to speed up the process. Firstly, the Housing Corporation must develop a positive strategy for assisting and supporting Black led Housing Associations in their attempts to provide accessible housing to the Black community in general and special groups within it in particular. There are five special groups who need attention. Each has a peculiar level of need. There are the elderly, the single parent, the disabled, the mentally ill and those returning to the community from custody.

The way in which the Housing Corporation handled the situation of the Harambee Housing Association raised great anxiety in the Black community of the Corporation's fairness and even a deep suspicion among many that there were unresolved elements of racism in the way some of the Corporation's officers behaved towards Harambee.

There is absolutely no justification for homelessness in this country. It is simply that the several agencies do not work together and that there is no coherent plan to tackle the problem. Without

115

being cynical it is easy to see how a Conservative government might be satisfied to see Labour run local authorities paying huge sums to private hoteliers and landlords rather than repairing housing stock and letting to people in need. The community must demand a comprehensive survey of accessible vacant properties in the hands of local government, central government departments (the MOD is a special case), agencies and private landlords with a view to making a concerted effort to ending homelessness once and for all.

HEALTH AND COMMUNITY CARE SERVICE

There is perhaps no service to which the Black community has contributed more than it has to the National Health Service. Many of the first Black immigrants came to Britain not only to improve their own lives but to answer a call, led by none other than Enoch Powell, then at the Ministry of Health to come and work in the National Health Service. It would be a pity if half a century or so later they found themselves in need of health care without a National Health Service to call on.

The Black community must rise up and defend the National Health Service against the current political rape which seeks to leave it ravaged of its pride of place as the most reliable and comprehensive care package anywhere in the world. Hospitals cannot be run like a network of motor car garages. A motor car left on a garage forecourt for a couple of days will still be there to be repaired. A heart patient left undiagnosed on an Accident & Emergency trolley while waiting for a bed may be dead by the time the bed is available. That patient could be you. The Black Agenda 2000 should place high priority on ensuring full accountability of the National Health Service and a return to a patient-comes-first ethos.

The arguments for Community Care Services are irrefutable. What is however needed is a resourced community to take on the responsibility of providing a sensitive and professionally adequate service. So far the central government has provided the logical arguments and left local government to find the resources. This cannot be accepted as a reasonable way to make progress. The Black community should continue to argue its case for resources and an involvement in community care planning and assessment.

ARTS AND BROADCASTING

One way in which society expresses the level of acceptance it affords to a migrant group is through the integration of its art into the fabric of the cultural life of the society. With the advent of huge sums of money pouring into the Arts from the National Lottery the Black community will be expecting that the imbalance in the support for ethnic minority arts will be addressed. No longer can excuses be condoned. Britain cannot claim to be a multi-racial society if it remains eurocentric in its art. It is important to restructure the Arts Council of Great Britain so it becomes more accountable to community aspirations and possessed of a greater vision of the cultural heritage of multi-racial Britain stretching beyond the Mediterranean and the Urals.

Black artists in both the performing and visual arts need to feel that public recognition is granted to their work, not on some insidious quota system of let a few through, but on the merit of their talents. All sectors of the Arts would need to review their role in promoting and maintaining open access to Black artists.

Broadcasting is central to presenting multi-racial Britain. The Black Agenda 2000 conscious of the work the BBC has put in as a Public Service broadcasting organisation would wish to support its continued charter, but would expect it to use its pole position to exert influence through example on the rest of the broadcasting industry. The Black community not only should be developing programmes for access to commercial broadcasting, but strategies to ensure that private sector broadcasting is responsive to community needs.

SPORTS AND RECREATION
The Black community has made a remarkable contribution to the nation's sports and recreation. There are still a few sports upon which it has not so far made a mark. These are those for which individual costs are great and for many in the community would be unsustainable. However, there still exists a perception within the committee rooms from which sports and recreation activities are controlled that the Black contribution (valued as it is for medals won) is a matter of brawn not brain. The experience of Devon Malcolm in South Africa during the 1995/96 winter cricket tour is a case in point. He was accused of being "a cricket non-entity" and not having "a cricket brain". Why did they pick him?

This is reflected in the fact that despite their contributions few come through to become coaches, managers or sports administrators. Agenda 2000 must now demand that the Sports Council perhaps with lottery funding should produce a scheme for developing Black coaches, managers and administrators.

CONCLUSION
The above agenda 2000 is by no means exhaustive. The Alliance of Black Organisations will doubtless as a result of their discussions and consultations make modifications, add other issues as experience at the time might dictate. Above all they will want to set

117

priorities for action, and look at ways in which they can be supportive to each other. Not all the Black communities are starting from the same point so it is essential to recognise that they will have different priorities. These should be openly recognised and respected allowing the Alliance to give its collective weight to advancing the themes that have been agreed. The Black community can no longer afford to support political parties that ignore their interests. Here starts the inclusive debate.

REFERENCES

CHAPTER ONE

1. Brian Elliott, David McCrowe and Frank Beckhofer. "Anxieties and Ambitions; the Petit Bourgeoisie and the New Right in Britain" Chapter 11, *Social Stratification and Economic Change*. Edited by David Rose. Hutchinson, London, 1988
2. Brian Elliott, David McCrowe and Frank Beckhofer. Ibid
3. Brian Elliott, David McCrowe and Frank Beckhofer. Ibid
4. Alan Howarth MP. "The Party Have Given Up On Fairness" *Independent*, 9 October 1995
5. Mathew D'Ancona. "Why I am a Christian" *Sunday Telegraph*, 7 April 1996

CHAPTER TWO

1. Paul Vallely. "Why this Man is Major's Nightmare" *Independent*, 12 March 1996
2. Paul Vallely. Ibid
3. Martin Bailey. "Only Blacks with a Share in the Stock Exchange" *Observer*, 21 September 1986
4. Colin Powell. *My American Journey*. Random House, New York, 1995
5. CRE. *Large Companies and Racial Equality*. London House, New York, 1995
6. Public Attitudes Survey Ltd. *Ethnic Origin Equal Opportunity Survey*. Employment Service Sheffield, 1993 p.1
7. Public Attitudes Survey Ltd. Ibid p.63
8. TGWU. *Equality for all. Winning Race Equality at Work*. London, 1991

CHAPTER THREE

1. Simon Pearce. "Swann and the Spirit of the Age" in *Anti-racism, an Assault on Education and Value*. The Sherwood Press, London, 1988
2. Simon Pearce. Ibid
3. Simon Pearce. Ibid
4. Dorothy Lepkowska. "Brixton School Beats Odds to go Top of the Class" *Evening Standard*, 31 January 1996
5. CRE. *Ethnic Minority School Teachers*. London, 1988

6. John Brennan and Philip McGrevor. *Employment of Graduates from Ethnic Minorities*. CRE, London, 1987
7. *Asian Times* "Another Blow for Muslim Schools" 4 March 1995
8. *Asian Times*. Ibid
9. *Asian Times*. Ibid
10. *Asian Times*. Ibid
11. CRE. *Annual Report 1989*.

CHAPTER FOUR

1. Susannah Strong. "Action, Not Words" *Community Care 27*, Oct-2 Nov 1994. p.14
2. The Audit Commission. *Finding A Place A Review of Mental Health Services for Adults*. HMSO, 1994
3. Glenda Cooper. "Mentally ill do better in Third World than in the West" *Independent*, 22 February 1996
4. Mike George. "A case for Optimism." Community Care, 14 May 1994
5. CRE. *Annual Report 1990*

CHAPTER FIVE

1. Nagal, S and Neif, M. "Racial Disparities That Supposedly Do Not Exist" *Notre Dame Law*. 52. 1976
2. Robert Waters. "Toward Multiracial Criminal Justice." *Justice of the Peace*. June 25 1988.
3. *Caribbean Times* "Don't Join Call by C10" 4 February 1982
4. Caroline Davies. "Yard Chief in Row Over Race" *Daily Telegraph*, 8 July 1995
5. Caroline Davies. Ibid
6. Caroline Davies. Ibid
7. Caroline Davies. Ibid
8. Caroline Davies. Ibid
9. Caroline Davies. Ibid
10. Valerie Elliot and Paul Goodman. "Focus Crime and Race" *Sunday Telegraph*, 9 July 1995
11. John Oakes. "Black Detective Wins £30,000 for Unfair Test" *Evening Standard*, 13 February 1996.
12. Jane Flanagan. "Police Target Jobless Blacks to Improve Ethnic Mix" *Sunday Telegraph*, 25 February 1996
13. Jane Flanagan. Ibid
14. Jane Flanagan. Ibid
15. Michael Swain. "Some Policemen are Racist Admits Condon" *Daily Express*, 3 April 1996

16. Roger Hood and Graca Cordovil. *Race and Sentencing.* Clarendon Press, Oxford, 1992
17. Bar Council. *Students' Guide to Equal Opportunities and Pupillage*, 1995
18. *Asian Times.* "Cowardly Screws and Twisted Inmates Terrorise Black Prisoners" 19 November 1994

CHAPTER SIX

1. Stuart Hall. "Viewpoint 2" *Multiracial Education Vol. 9 No.2*, Spring 1981
2. I Taylor and A Clarke. "Law and Order Politics, Television and the 1979 Election" in *Law and Order.* Project, Occasional Paper 1, University of Sheffield, Centre for Criminological and Socio-legal Studies, June 1980
3. CRE. "Radio for Ethnic and Linquistic Minorities." *CRE Conference Report*, London, 1990
4. Bennett Will. "Condon Accuses Black Newspaper Over Brixton Riot" *Independent*, 27 January 1996

CHAPTER SEVEN

1. *Asian Times.* "Major Told to Open Borders" 1 April 1995
2. Nick Cohen. "Britain Bars All Nigerian Refugees" *Independent*, 24 March 1996
3. CRE. *Second Review of the Race Relations Act 1976*, London, 1991
4. Black Rights (UK). *Black People, Human Rights and the Media*, London, 1989
5. *Independent.* "Far from the Promised Land" 10 October 1995
6. *Independent.* Ibid.

BIBLIOGRAPHY

Amin, K and   *Poverty in Black and White, and Ethnic*
Oppenheim, C.   *Minorities Deprivation.* The Runnymede
Trust, London, 1992

Bagley, C and   "Policy Dilemmas and the Adoption of
Young, L. ed.   Black Children" in *Social Work and Ethnicity*,
Cheltham 1982

Baker, Bob et al.   *Read All About It: A Study of Race Reporting
in Newspapers.* AFFOR, Birmingham, 1980

Berlin, Ira et al.   *Free At Last.* The New Press, New York; 1992

Berry, D.   *Society Tomorrow: Taking the Strain*, The
Guardian, 30 October 1985

Bowser, Benjamin   *Impacts of Racism on White Americans.*
P. and Hunt,   Sage Publishing, Newbury Park, California,
Raymond (eds)   1981

Britton, Arthur and *Racism, Sexism and Oppression*, Basil
Maynard   Blackwell, Oxford, 1984

Brooking, C. Foster *Teaching for Equality: Education Resources on
and Smith, S.   Race and Gender.* Runnymede Trust, London,
1987

Brown, C.   *Black and White Britain: The Third P.S.I.
Study.* Heineman, London, 1984

Brown, C.,   *Spanner In The Works: Education for Racial
Banfield, J. and   Equality and Social Justice in White Schools.*
Stone, M.   Trentham Books, London, 1981

Brown, S.C.   *Objectivity and Cultural Divergence.*
Cambridge University Press, Cambridge, 1984

Butcher, H. (ed).   *Community and Public Policy*, Pluto Press,
London: 1994

CNAA Development Services	*Higher Education and the Labour Market.* Working Paper. 1. 1985
Commission for Racial Equality	*Local Authorities and Racial Equality, A Summary Report*, London: 1995
	Racial Equality Means Business: A Standard for Racial Equality for Employers. London: 1995
	Racial Equality Means Quality: A Standard for Racial Equality for Local Government. London: 1995
	Black and Ethnic Minority Women and Men London: 1994
	Lessons of the Law: A Casebook of Racial Discrimination in Education. London: 1991
	Living in Terror: A Report on Racial Violence and Harassment in Housing. London: 1987
	NHS contracts and Racial Equality: A Guide. London: 1991
	A Question of Judgement. London 1992
	Adopting a Better Policy: Adoption and Fostering of Ethnic Minority Children. London: 1990
Croft, M and Croft, A.	"The Participation of Ethnic Minorities in Further and Higher Education" in *Educational Research Vol. 21*, 1983
D.E.S.	*West Indian Children in Our Schools. The Rampton Report.* The Rampton Report, HMSO: London: 1981
Dummett, Ann	*A Portrait of English Racism.* Caraf Publications, London: 1984

126

Echiejile, Innocent A.   *Equal Opportunities: Recruitment and Selection.* The Book Guild, Sussex: 1992

Equal Opportunities Commission   Equal Opportunities: A Guide for Employers. E.O.C. Manchester: 1988

Fitzgerald, Marian   *Political Parties and Black People* Runnymede Trust, London: 1984

George, V and Miller, S.   Social Policy Towards 2000. Routledge, London: 1994

Haynes, Aaron C.W.   *The State of Black Britain Vol 1*, Root Publishing, London: 1983

Hepple, B.   *Race, Jobs and The Law in Britain* Penguin, Harmondsworth: 1970

Home Office   *Racial Attacks: Report of A Home Office Study.* HMSO, London: 1981

Racial Discrimination: A Guide to Race Relations Act 1976. HMSO, London: 1977

Husbands, Charles   *White Media and Black Britain.* Arrow Books, London: 1973

IPM   *The IPM Equal Opportunities Code.* London: 1990

Jones, K.   *Asylum and After.* Athlone Press, London: 1994

Jones, T.   *Britain's Ethnic Minorities: An Analysis of the Labour Force Survey.* Policy Studies Institute. London: 1993

Schwartz, Barney N., and Disch, Robert   *White Racism: Its History, Pathology and Practice.* Dell Publishing Co., New York: 1970

Simons, Ken   *Citizen Advocacy: The Inside View.* University of Bristol, Bristol: 1994

Siraj - Blatchford, I   "A Study of Black Students' Perceptions
                         of Racism" in *Initial Teacher Education,*
                         Bristol Educational Research Journal.
                         Vol 17. No 1. 1991

Smith, D.   *Overseas Doctors in the National Health*
                        Service. Heinemann. London 1980

Troyna, B and   *Racism in Children's Lives: A Study*
Hatsher, R.   *of Mainly White Primary Schools.*
                        Routledge London: 1992

Wainwright, D.   "A Programme for Change" in
                        Discrimination and Disadvantage in
                        Employment: The Experience of Black
                        Workers. P. Braham et al. (ed) Harper
                        & Row. London: 1986

Wiley, Ralph   *What Black People Should Do Now.*
                        Bullantine Books, New York: 1994

Wright, C.   *Race Relations in the Primary School*
                        David Fulton Publishers. London: 1992